DowningStreetGate

The Dodgiest Dossier

SPOKESMAN
for the
Bertrand Russell Peace Foundation

First published in 2005 by
Spokesman,
Russell House, Bulwell Lane
Nottingham NG6 0BT
Phone 0115 970 8318   Fax 0115 942 0433
e-mail elfeuro@compuserve.com
www.spokesmanbooks.com

ISBN 0 85124 712 1

A CIP catalogue is available from the British Library

Printed by the Russell Press Ltd (phone 0115 978 4505)

CONTENTS

Foreword by Ken Coates		5
The Dodgiest Dossier		9
Edited by Tony Simpson		
with grateful acknowledgements to Glen Rangwala		
I	Iraq: Options Paper	11
II	Iraq: Legal Background	24
III	Sir David Manning's Advice to the Prime Minister	30
IV	Sir Christopher Meyer's Note of His Meeting with Paul Wolfowitz	33
V	Advice to Jack Straw	36
VI	Straw's Advice to Blair	39
VII	Iraq: Conditions for Military Action	42
VIII	Iraq: Prime Minister's Meeting, 23 July 2002 ('The Downing Street Memo')	50
IX	An Early Start to the Air War	54
X	The Attorney General's Legal Advice	58
XI	A Principled Resignation	75
Afterword: Questions for President Bush by Representative John Conyers, Jr. and others		77

Foreword
by Ken Coates

In August 2004 Adam Price, the Member of Parliament for Carmarthen East and Dinefwr, and spokesman of Plaid Cymru, first published his report on the potential impeachment of Prime Minister Blair for High Crimes and Misdemeanours in relation to the invasion of Iraq. In October, we brought out this text as a little book, under the title *A Case to Answer*. The indictment was prepared by Glen Rangwala and Dan Plesch. It remains a very solid document, and is still much in demand.

Mr. Blair is never unduly self-critical, and during his dispute in the European Council of Ministers, in June 2005, he was able to demonstrate his imperviousness to justified reproach once again. Speaking to the European Parliament, on the rejection of the proposed European Constitution, he said on the 23rd June, that European statesmen should listen to the clamour of the opposition. 'It is time to give ourselves a reality check' he said. 'The people are blowing trumpets around the city walls. Are we listening?'

Many of us remember the day when the British people were sounding the trumpets not around the city walls, but inside the citadel, in the great demonstration which protested against the coming war on Iraq. At least one million, and many claim, two million people, flocked into the capital to tell the Prime Minister that he had no right to go to war. 'Not in our name' they said.

We now know that the powerful hostility of so many British people was in fact matched by an important part (dare we say the most honourable part?) of the political establishment. Senior officials, intelligence personnel and diplomats shared in the disquiet of the populace. But Mr. Blair did not. His mission was to lead, whether those he expected to follow liked it or not.

Adam Price's brave initiative has not yet brought about the impeachment of Mr. Blair, although many of us think that if there were any justice in the world it should do so.

However, there is now a lively possibility of the impeachment of President Bush, which arises from the publication of the briefing papers which were leaked in the *Sunday Times* immediately before the British General Election on 5 May. These papers showed in graphic detail how weak was the pre-war evidence for attacking Iraq. They revealed that the Americans had no clear plan for the occupation of Iraq, and that the Bush administration lacked realism about the likely post-war situation. The briefing papers made the bald claim that 'the intelligence and facts were being fixed around the policy'. They reveal that the British Government knew that there was no major threat from weapons of mass destruction in Iraq, and they also knew that the claim that Iraq had links with al Qaeda was 'frankly unconvincing'.

Most of these papers were prepared during 2002. That July, the head of British Intelligence, Sir Richard Dearlove, read into the minutes to the Prime Minister and Jack Straw that President Bush had already decided to attack Iraq. This was some months before the President took the question of Iraq to the United Nations, and during the time that Mr. Bush told both Congress and the wider public that he had no plans for an attack. And all the time the Prime Minister was denying that any decision had yet been taken for an invasion. Indeed, on the day after that meeting – 24 July – Blair told the House of Commons in response to a question from Diane Abbott that 'we have not yet reached the point of decision ... How we deal with [Iraq's weapons] is an open question'. A few moments later, he said in response to a question from Tam Dalyell that 'we have not taken the decision to commit British forces'. Blair continued to tell the Commons and the public for the next eight months that he had not committed himself to invading Iraq, and that he was continuing to sift through the evidence before coming to a final decision. The minutes of the 23 July 2002 meeting demonstrate that this process of public deliberation was no more than an elaborate charade.

The July minutes also reveal how the key players recognised that the information about Iraq's weapons was clearly dodgy. MI6's Richard Dearlove told Blair that 'Bush wanted to remove Saddam ... justified by the conjunction of terrorism and WMD. But the intelligence and facts were being fixed around the policy'. In other words, the Americans had already decided upon the excuse; they just needed to fabricate the evidence for it. Jack Straw added 'the case [for war] was thin. Saddam was not threatening his neighbours, and his

WMD capability was less than that of Libya, North Korea or Iran'. In direct contrast with the position Straw provided in private, Blair continued to talk of a 'threat' from Iraq. He told a press conference six weeks after the meeting that 'Iraq poses a real and a unique threat to the security of the region and the rest of the world.' The gap between these statements could hardly be wider.

On the 26th July 2002 Clare Short recorded that she raised her concern about Iraq in a meeting with Blair. She wanted a debate in Cabinet: but he said it was unnecessary ... nothing had been decided and would not be over the summer. As late as the 9th September 2002 Short's diary records:

> 'T[ony] B[lair] gave me assurances when I asked for Iraq to be discussed at Cabinet that no decision made and not imminent.'

The first of these leaked papers was published in the *Daily Telegraph* on 18 September 2004. The rest were published in the *Sunday Times* on 1st May 2005 and in subsequent numbers of the journal, and on the *Sunday Times* website. The papers have aroused enormous interest in the United States, and have given rise to a petition which has gathered hundreds of thousands of signatures (see p.77). Representative John Conyers Jnr, a Michigan Democrat, wrote to the President with a series of questions about the Downing Street memorandum. Eighty-eight other members of Congress quickly endorsed this letter.

The Downing Street minutes reveal how duplicitous has been the published record of the British Government, in addition to arousing such justified concern in the United States. They should be set against the public record, which includes the infamous dodgy dossier, published with such a fanfare to soften up public opinion for the ongoing offensive.

In making these papers available, those who released them have shown how desperately damaging the official record truly is. Here, indeed, we have the dodgiest dossier of all.

THE DODGIEST DOSSIER

The papers have been amended to correct obvious literal mistakes and to spell out acronyms.

I
Options for Iraq

There was a flurry of activity in Downing Street at the beginning of March 2002, a full year before the war on Iraq officially commenced. In January, President Bush had made his 'Axis of Evil' State of the Union address, naming Iraq, Iran and North Korea. Prime Minister Blair was due to visit the President at his ranch in Crawford, Texas, in April. An 'Iraq: Options Paper' supplemented with 'Legal Background' discussed the possibilities.

8 March 2002

SECRET UK EYES ONLY

IRAQ: OPTIONS PAPER

SUMMARY
Since 1991, our objective has been to re-integrate a law-abiding Iraq which does not possess weapons of mass destruction or threaten its neighbours, into the international community. Implicitly, this cannot occur with Saddam Hussein in power. As a least worst option, we have supported a policy of containment which has been partially successful. However:
- Despite sanctions, Iraq continues to develop weapons of mass destruction, although our intelligence is poor. Saddam has used weapons of mass destruction in the past and could do so again if his regime were threatened, though there is no greater threat now than in recent years that Saddam will use weapons of mass destruction; and
- Saddam's brutal regime remains in power and destabilises the Arab and wider Islamic world.

We have two options. We could toughen the existing containment policy. This would increase the pressure on Saddam. It would not reintegrate Iraq into the international community.

The US administration has lost faith in containment and is now considering regime change. The end states could either be a Sunni strongman or a representative government.

The three options for achieving regime change are:
- covert support to opposition groups to mount an uprising / coup;
- air support for opposition groups to mount an uprising / coup; and
- a full-scale ground campaign.

These are not mutually exclusive. Options 1 and/or 2 would be natural precursors to Option 3. The greater investment of Western forces, the greater our control over Iraq's future, but the greater the cost and the longer we would need to stay. The only certain means to remove Saddam and his elite is to invade and impose a new government, but this could involve nation building over many years. Even a representative government could seek to acquire weapons of mass destruction and build-up its conventional forces, so long as Iran and Israel retain their weapons of mass destruction and conventional armouries and there was no acceptable solution to Palestinian grievances.

A legal justification for invasion would be needed. Subject to Law Officers advice, none currently exists. This makes moving quickly to invade legally very difficult. We should therefore consider a staged approach, establishing international support, building up pressure on Saddam, and developing military plans. There is a lead time of about 6 months to a ground offensive.

CURRENT OBJECTIVES OF UK POLICY

1. Within our objectives of preserving peace and stability in the Gulf and ensuring energy security, our current objectives towards Iraq are:
- the reintegration of a law-abiding Iraq which does not possess weapons of mass destruction or threaten its neighbours, into the international community. Implicitly, this cannot occur with Saddam in power; and
- hence, as the least worst option, we have supported containment of Iraq, by constraining Saddam's ability to re-arm or build up weapons of mass destruction and to threaten his neighbours.

2. Subsidiary objectives are:
- Preserving the territorial integrity of Iraq;
- improving the humanitarian situation of the Iraqi people;
- protecting the Kurds in Northern Iraq;

- sustaining UK/US co-operation, including, if necessary, by moderating US policy; and
- maintaining the credibility and authority of the Security Council.

HAS CONTAINMENT WORKED?

3. Since 1991, the policy of containment has been partially successful:
- Sanctions have effectively frozen Iraq's nuclear programme;
- Iraq has been prevented from rebuilding its conventional arsenal to pre-Gulf War levels;
- ballistic missile programmes have been severely restricted;
- Biological weapons (BW) and Chemical Weapons (CW) programmes have been hindered;
- No Fly Zones established over northern and southern Iraq have given some protection to the Kurds and the Shia. Although subject to continuing political pressure, the Kurds remain autonomous; and
- Saddam has not succeeded in seriously threatening his neighbours.

4. However:
- Iraq continues to develop weapons of mass destruction, although our intelligence is poor. Iraq has up to 20 650km-range missiles left over from the Gulf War. These are capable of hitting Israel and the Gulf states. Design work for other ballistic missiles over the UN limit of 150km continues. Iraq continues with its biological weapons and chemical weapons programmes and, if it has not already done so, could produce significant quantities of biological weapons agents within days and chemical weapons agent within weeks of a decision to do so. We believe it could deliver chemical and biological weapons by a variety of means, including in ballistic missile warheads. There are also some indications of a continuing nuclear programme. Saddam has used weapons of mass destruction in the past and could do so again if his regime were threatened.
- Saddam leads a brutal regime, which impoverishes his people. While in power Saddam is a rallying point for anti-Western sentiment in the Arab and wider Islamic world, and as such a cause of instability; and
- despite UN controls over Iraq's oil revenue under Oil for Food, there is considerable oil and other smuggling.

5. In this context, and against the background of our desire to re-

integrate a law-abiding Iraq into the international community, we examine the two following policy options:
- a toughening of the existing containment policy, facilitated by 11 September; and
- regime change by military means: a new departure which would require the construction of a coalition and a legal justification.

TOUGHENING CONTAINMENT

6. This would consist of the following elements:
- full implementation of all relative UN Security Council Resolutions, particularly 687 (1991) and 1284 (1999). We should ensure that the Goods Review List (GRL) is introduced in May and that Russia holds to its promise not to block. The signs are positive but continuing pressure is needed. (The Goods Review List focuses sanctions exclusively on preventing shipments of weapons of mass destruction-related and other arms, while allowing other business without scrutiny. As such, it will greatly facilitate legitimate Iraqi commerce under Oil for Food.);
- encourage the United States not to block discussions to clarify the modalities of Resolution 1284 once Russian agreement to the Goods Review List has been secured. We should take a hard-line on each area for clarification – the purpose of clarification is not to lower the bar on Iraqi compliance; but
- Permanent 5 and Security Council unity would facilitate a specific demand that Iraq re-admit the UN inspectors. Our aim would be to tell Saddam to admit inspectors or face the risk of military action.
- push for tougher action (especially by the United States) against states breaking sanctions. This should not discriminate between allies (Turkey), friends (United Arab Emirates) and others (especially Syria). It would put real pressure on Saddam either to submit to meaningful inspections or to lash out;
- maintain our present military posture, including in the no fly zones, and be prepared to respond robustly to any Iraqi adventurism, and
- continue to make clear (without overtly espousing regime change) our view that Iraq would be better off without Saddam. We could trail the rosy future for Iraq without him in a 'Contract with the Iraqi People', although to be at all credible, this would need some detailed work.

The Dodgiest Dossier

7. What it could achieve:
- There will be greater pressure on Saddam. The Goods Review List will make sanctions more attractive to at least some of their detractors. Improving implementation of sanctions would reduce the regime's illicit revenues; and
- the return of UN weapons inspectors would allow greater scrutiny of Iraqi weapons of mass destruction programmes and of Iraqi forces in general. If they found significant evidence of weapons of mass destruction, were expelled or, in face of an ultimatum, not re-admitted in the first place, then this could provide legal justification for large-scale military action (see below).

8. But:
- Some of the difficulties with the existing policy still apply;
- those states in breach of sanctions will want compensation if they are to change tack;
- Saddam is only likely to permit the return of inspectors if he believes the threat of large scale US military action is imminent and that such concessions would prevent the United States from acting decisively. Playing for time, he would then embark on a renewed policy of non-co-operation; and
- although containment has held for the past decade, Iraq has progressively increased its international engagement. Even if the Goods Review List makes sanctions more sustainable, the sanctions regime could collapse in the long term.

9. Tougher containment would not re-integrate Iraq into the international community as it offers little prospect of removing Saddam. He will continue with his weapons of mass destruction programmes, destabilising the Arab and Islamic world, and impoverishing his people. But there is no greater threat now that he will use weapons of mass destruction than there has been in recent years, so continuing containment is an option.

US VIEWS

10. The United States has lost confidence in containment. Some in government want Saddam removed. The success of Operation

Enduring Freedom, distrust of UN sanctions and inspection regimes, and unfinished business from 1991 are all factors. Washington believes the legal basis for an attack on Iraq already exists. Nor will it necessarily be governed by wider political factors. The United States may be willing to work with a much smaller coalition than we think desirable.

REGIME CHANGE
11. In considering the options for regime change below, we need to first consider what sort of Iraq we want? There are two possibilities;
● A Sunni military strongman. He would be likely to maintain Iraqi territorial integrity. Assistance with reconstruction and political rehabilitation could be traded for assurances on abandoning weapons of mass destruction programmes and respecting human rights, particularly of ethnic minorities. The United States and other militaries could withdraw quickly. However, there would then be a strong risk of the Iraqi system reverting to type. Military coup could succeed coup until an autocratic, Sunni dictator emerged who protected Sunni interests. With time he could acquire weapons of mass destruction; or
● a representative broadly democratic government. This would be Sunni-led but, within a federal structure, the Kurds would be guaranteed autonomy and the Shia access to government. Such a regime would be less likely to develop weapons of mass destruction and threaten its neighbours. However, to survive it would require the United States and others to commit to nation building for many years. This would entail a substantial international security force and help with reconstruction.

OTHER FACTORS TO CONSIDER: INTERNAL
12. Saddam has a strong grip on power maintained through fear and patronage. The security and intelligence apparatus, including the Republican and Special Republican Guard, who protect the regime so effectively are predominantly drawn from the Arab Sunni minority (20 – 25 per cent of the population); many from Tikrit like Saddam. They fear non-Sunni rule, which would bring retribution and the end of their privileges. The regime's success in defeating the 1991

uprising stemmed from senior Sunni officers looking into the abyss of Shia rule and preserving their interests by backing Saddam. In the current circumstances, a military revolt or coup is a remote possibility.
13. Unaided, the Iraqi opposition is incapable of overthrowing the regime. The external opposition is weak, divided and lacks domestic credibility. The predominant group is the Iraqi National Congress (INC), an umbrella organisation led by Ahmad Chalabi, a Shia and convicted fraudster, popular on Capitol Hill. The other major group, the Iraqi National Accord (INA) espouses moderate Arab socialism and is led by another Shia, Ayad Allawi. Neither group has a military capability and both are badly penetrated by Iraqi intelligence. In 1996, a CIA attempt to stir the opposition groups ended in wholesale executions. Most Iraqis see the INC/INA as Western stooges.

14. The internal opposition is small and fractured on ethnic and sectarian grounds. There is no effective Sunni Arab opposition. There are 3-4 million Kurds in northern Iraq. Most live in the Kurdish Autonomous Zone, established in 1991. The Kurds deploy at least 40,000 lightly armed militia but are divided between two main parties, the Patriotic Union of Kurdistan (PUK) and the Kurdistan Democratic Party (KDP). These groups have an interest in preserving the status quo and are more interested in seeking advantage over the other than allying against Saddam. Divide and rule is easy; in 1996 the KDP assisted the Iraqi Army's expulsion of the PUK and the Iraqi opposition groups from Irbil.

15. The Kurds do not co-operate with the Shia Arabs who form 60 per cent of the population. The main Shia opposition group is the Supreme Council for the Islamic Revolution in Iraq (SCIRI), with 3-5,000 fighters, but it is tainted by Iranian support. Most Shia would like to have a greater say in Iraqi government, but not necessarily control: they do not want secession, Islamic autonomy or Iranian influence.

REGIONAL
16. Iraq's neighbours have a direct interest in the country's affairs. Iran and Turkey, in particular, are wary of US influence and

oppose some opposition groups. Turkey, conscious of its own restive Kurdish minority, will do anything to prevent the establishment of an independent Kurdish state in northern Iraq, including intervention. Iran, also with a Kurdish minority, would also oppose a Kurdish state and is keen to protect the rights of its co-religionists in the south (see Foreign and Commonwealth Office paper on Permanent 5, European and regional views of possible military action against Iraq, attached.)

17. We have looked at three options for achieving a regime change (we dismissed assassination of Saddam Hussein as an option because it would be illegal):

OPTION 1: COVERT SUPPORT TO OPPOSITION GROUPS
18. The aim would be to bring down the regime by internal revolt, aided by the defection or at least acquiescence of large sections of the Army. A group of Sunni generals probably from within the Republican Guard, might depose Saddam if they decided the alternative was defeat. This option could be pursued by providing covert intelligence, large scale financial and Special Forces support to opposition groups. The Kurds would be persuaded to unite and attack into northern Iraq, tying down some Iraqi forces. Simultaneously, in a greater threat to the regime, the Shia would rise up in the southern cities, and in Baghdad.

19. This option also has a very low prospect of success on its own. The external opposition is not strong enough to overthrow Saddam and would be rejected by most Iraqis as a replacement government. The Kurds could only mount a very limited offensive in the north. Mass uprisings in the south would be unlikely. The US failure to support the 1991 uprising remains vivid. The Republican Guard would move against any opposition and any wavering regular Army units. There would also be a high risk of US/coalition forces being captured, buttressing Saddam and his reputation as Arab folk hero. On the other hand, this option has never been pursued in a concerted, single-minded way before and should not be dismissed, at least as a possible precursor to Options 2 and 3.

OPTION 2: AN AIR CAMPAIGN PROVIDING OVERT SUPPORT TO OPPOSITION GROUPS LEADING TO A COUP OR UPRISING
20. The aim would be to assist an internal revolt by providing strategic and tactical air support for opposition groups to move against the regime. Such support would disable Saddam's military and security apparatus. Suspected weapons of mass destruction facilities would also be targeted. Substantial numbers of aircraft and munitions would need to be built up in theatre over a period of months. Any campaign would take several weeks at least, probably several months. Pressure on the regime could be increased by massing ground and naval forces and threatening a land invasion.

21. This operation has no guarantee of success. The build up of pressure might persuade other Sunnis to overthrow Saddam and his family, but there is no guarantee that another Sunni autocrat would be better. Comparisons with Afghanistan are misleading. Saddam's military and security apparatus is considerably more potent and cohesive. We are not aware of any Karzai figure able to command respect inside and outside Iraq. Arab states would only back the plan if they were sure Saddam would be deposed. At least the co-operation of Kuwait would be needed for the necessary military build-up. The Arab street would oppose an air attack against Iraq, but visibility of a popular uprising could calm Arab public opinion.

OPTION 3: A GROUND CAMPAIGN
22. The aim would be to launch a full-scale ground offensive to destroy Saddam's military machine and remove him from power. A pro-Western regime would be installed which would destroy Iraq's weapons of mass destruction capability, make peace with Iraq's neighbours and give rights to all Iraqis, including ethnic minorities. As in the Gulf War, this would need to be preceded by a major air-offensive to soften up defences.

23. US contingency planning prior to 11 September indicated that such a ground campaign would require 200-400,000 troops. The numbers would be roughly half those of 1991 because Iraqi forces are now considerably weaker. Any invasion force would need to pose a

credible threat to Baghdad in order to persuade members of the Sunni military elite that their survival was better served by deserting to the coalition than staying loyal to Saddam. Sufficient air assets would need three months and ground forces at least four-five months to assemble, so on logistical grounds a ground campaign is not feasible until autumn 2002. The optimal times to start action are early spring ... Eid festival. [11 February 2003]

24. From a purely military perspective it would be very difficult to launch an invasion from Kuwait alone. Carrier-based aircraft would not be enough because of the need for land-based air-to-air refuelling. To be confident of success, bases either in Jordan or in Saudi Arabia would be required. However, a wider and durable international coalition would be advantageous for both military and political reasons. Securing moderate Arab support would be greatly assisted by the promise of a quick and decisive campaign, and credible action by the United States to address the Middle East Peace Process.

25. The risks include US and others military casualties. Any coalition would need much tending over the difficult months of preparation for an actual invasion. Iran, fearing further US encirclement and that it will be invaded next, will be prickly but is likely to remain neutral. With his regime in danger, Saddam could use weapons of mass destruction, either before or during an invasion. Saddam could also target Israel as he did during the Gulf War. Restraining Israel will be difficult. It could try to pre-empt a weapons of mass destruction attack and has certainly made clear that it would retaliate. Direct Israeli military involvement in Iraq would greatly complicate coalition management and risk spreading conflict more widely.

26. None of the above options is mutually exclusive. Options 1 and/or 2 would be natural precursors to Option 3. All options have lead times. If an invasion is contemplated this autumn, then a decision will need to be taken in principle six months in advance. The greater investment of Western forces, the greater our control over Iraq's future, but the greater the cost and the longer we would need to stay. Option 3 comes closest to guaranteeing regime change. At this stage

we need to wait to see which option or combination of options may be favoured by the US government.

27. But it should be noted that even a representative government could seek to acquire weapons of mass destruction and build-up its conventional forces, so long as Iran and Israel retain their weapons of mass destruction and conventional armouries.

LEGAL CONSIDERATIONS

28. A full opinion should be sought from the Law Officers if the above options are developed further. But in summary, CONTAINMENT generally involves the implementation of existing UN Security Council Resolutions and has a firm legal foundation. Of itself, REGIME CHANGE has no basis in international law. A separate note by Foreign and Commonwealth Office Legal Advisors setting out the general legal background and the obligations in the relevant UN Resolutions is attached.

29. In the judgement of the Joint Intelligence Committee there is no recent evidence of Iraq complicity with international terrorism. There is therefore no justification for action against Iraq based on action in self-defence (Article 51) to combat imminent threats of terrorism as in Afghanistan. However, Article 51 would come into play if Iraq were about to attack a neighbour.

30. Currently, offensive military action against Iraq can only be justified if Iraq is held to be in breach of the Gulf War ceasefire resolution, 687. 687 imposed obligations on Iraq with regard to the elimination of weapons of mass destruction and monitoring these obligations. But 687 never terminated the authority to use force mandated in UN Security Council Resolution 678 (1990). Thus a violation of 687 can revive the authorisation to use force in 678.

31. As the ceasefire was proclaimed by the Security Council in 687, it is for the Council to decide whether a breach of obligations has occurred. There is a precedent. UN Security Council Resolution 1205 (1998), passed after the expulsion of the UN inspectors, stated that in doing so Iraq had acted in flagrant violation of its obligations under

687. In our view, this revived the authority for the use of force under 678 and underpinned Operation Desert Fox. In contrast to general legal opinion, the US asserts the right of individual Member States to determine whether Iraq has breached 687, regardless of whether the Council has reached this assessment.

32. For the Permanent 5 and the majority of the Council to take the view that Iraq was in breach of 687:
- they would need to be convinced that Iraq was in breach of its obligations regarding weapons of mass destruction, and ballistic missiles. Such proof would need to be incontrovertible and of large-scale activity. Current intelligence is insufficiently robust to meet this criterion. Even with overriding proof China, France and Russia, in particular, would need considerable lobbying to approve or acquiesce in a new resolution authorising military action against Iraq. Concessions in other policy areas might be needed. However, many Western states, at least, would not wish to oppose the United States on such a major issue: or
- if Permanent 5 unity could be obtained, Iraq refused to re-admit UN inspectors after a clear ultimatum by the UN Security Council; or
- the UN inspectors were re-admitted to Iraq and found sufficient evidence of weapons of mass destruction activity or were again expelled trying to do so.

CONCLUSION
33. In sum, despite the considerable difficulties, the use of overriding force in a ground campaign is the only option that we can be confident will remove Saddam and bring Iraq back into the international community.
34. To launch such a campaign would require a staged approach:
- winding up the pressure: increasing the pressure on Saddam through tougher containment. Stricter implementation of sanctions and a military build-up will frighten his regime. A refusal to admit UN inspectors, or their admission and subsequent likely frustration, which resulted in an appropriate finding by the Security Council, could provide the justification for military action. Saddam would try to prevent this, although he has miscalculated before;

- careful planning: detailed military planning on the various invasion and basing options, and when appropriate force deployment;
- coalition building: diplomatic work to establish an international coalition to provide the broadest political and military support to a ground campaign. This will need to focus on China, France and particularly Russia who have the ability to block action in the UN Security Council and on the other Europeans. Special attention will need to be paid to moderate Arab states and to Iran;
- incentives: as an incentive guarantees will need to be made with regard to Iraqi territorial integrity. Plans should be worked up in advance of the great benefits the international community could provide for a post-Saddam Iraq and its people. These should be published.
- tackling other regional issues: an effort to engage the United States in a serious effort to re-energise the Middle East Peace Process would greatly assist coalition building; and
- sensitising the public: a media campaign to warn of the dangers that Saddam poses and to prepare public opinion both in the United Kingdom and abroad.

35. The US should be encouraged to consult widely on its plans.

OVERSEAS AND DEFENCE SECRETARIAT
CABINET OFFICE
8 MARCH 2002

II
Legal Background

Also dated 8 March 2002, this is the note from the Foreign and Commonwealth Office legal advisors referred to in paragraph 28 of the Options Paper, 'setting out the general legal back-ground and the obligations in the relevant UN Resolutions'.

CONFIDENTIAL

IRAQ: LEGAL BACKGROUND
(i) Use of Force: (a) Security Council Resolutions
                (b) Self-defence
                (c) Humanitarian Intervention
(ii) No Fly Zones
(iii) Security Council Resolutions relevant to the sanctions regime
(iv) Security Council Resolutions relating to the United Nations Monitoring, Verification and Inspection Commission (UNMOVIC)

(I) USE OF FORCE: (A) SECURITY COUNCIL RESOLUTIONS RELEVANT TO THE AUTHORISATION OF THE USE OF FORCE
1. Following its invasion and annexation of Kuwait, the Security Council authorised the use of force against Iraq in resolution 675 (1990); this resolution authorised coalition forces to use all necessary means to force Iraq to withdraw, and to restore international peace and security in the area. This resolution gave a legal basis for Operation Desert Storm, which was brought to an end by the cease-fire set out by the Council in resolution 687 (1991). The conditions for the cease-fire in that resolution (and subsequent resolutions) imposed obligations on Iraq with regard to the elimination of weapons of mass destruction and monitoring of its obligations. Resolution 687 (1991) suspended but did not terminate the authority to use force in resolution 678 (1990).

2. In the United Kingdom's view a violation of Iraq's obligations which undermines the basis of the cease-fire in resolution 687 (1991) can revive the authorisation to use force in resolution 678 (1990). As the cease-fire was proclaimed by the Council in resolution 687 (1991), it is for the Council to assess whether any such breach of those obligations

has occurred. The United States have a rather different view: they maintain that the assessment of breach is for individual member States. We are not aware of any other State which supports this view.

3. The authorisation to use force contained in resolution 678 (1990) has been revived in this way on certain occasions. For example, when Iraq refused to cooperate with the UN Special Commission (UNSCOM) in 1997/8, a series of Security Council Resolutions condemned the decision as unacceptable. In resolution 1205 (1998) the Council condemned Iraq's decision to end all cooperation with the UN Special Commission as a flagrant violation of Iraq's obligations under resolution 687 (1991), and restated that the effective operation of the UN Special Commission was essential for the implementation of that Resolution. In our view these resolutions had the effect of causing the authorisation to use force in resolution 678 (1991) to revive, which provided a legal basis for Operation Desert Fox. In a letter to the President of the Security Council in 1998 we stated that the objective of that operation was to seek compliance by Iraq with the obligations laid down by the Council that the operation was undertaken only when it became apparent that there was no other way of achieving compliance by Iraq, and that the action was limited to what was necessary to secure this objective.

4. The more difficult issue is whether we are still able to rely on the same legal base for the use of force more than three years after the adoption of resolution 1205 (1998). Military action in 1998 (and on previous occasions) followed on from specific decisions of the Council; there has now not been any significant decision by the Council since 1998. Our interpretation of resolution 1205 was controversial anyway; many of our partners did not think the legal basis was sufficient as the authority to use force was not explicit. Reliance on it now would be unlikely to receive any support.

USE OF FORCE: (B) SELF-DEFENCE
5. The conditions that have to be met for the exercise of the right of self-defence are well-known:
i) There must be an armed attack upon a State or such an attack must be imminent;

ii) The use of force must be necessary and other means to reverse/avert the attack must be unavailable;
iii) The acts in self-defence must be proportionate and strictly confined to the object of stopping the attack.

The right of self-defence may only be exercised until the Security Council has taken measures necessary to ensure international peace and security and anything done in exercise of the right of self-defence must be immediately reported to the Council.

6. For the exercise of the right of self-defence there must be more than 'a threat'. There has to be an armed attack actual or imminent. The development of possession of nuclear weapons does not in itself amount to an armed attack; what would be needed would be clear evidence of an imminent attack. During the Cold War there was certainly a threat in the sense that various States had nuclear weapons which they might, at short notice unleash upon each other. But that did not mean the mere possession of nuclear weapons, or indeed their possession in time of high tension or attempt to obtain them, was sufficient to justify pre-emptive action. And when Israel attacked an Iraqi nuclear reactor, near Baghdad, on 7 June 1981 it was 'strongly condemned' by the Security Council (acting unanimously) as a 'military' attack ... in clear violation of the Charter of the United Nations and the norms of international conduct'.

USE OF FORCE: (C) HUMANITARIAN INTERVENTION
7. In the United Kingdom's view the use of force may be justified if the action is taken to prevent an overwhelming humanitarian catastrophe. The limits to this highly contentious doctrine are not clearly defined, but we would maintain the catastrophe must be clear and well documented, that there must be no other means short of the use of force which could prevent it, and that the measures taken must be proportionate. This doctrine partly underlies the very limited action taken by allied aircraft to patrol the No Fly Zones in Iraq (following action by Saddam to repress the Kurds and the Shia in the early 90s), which involved occasional and limited use of force by those aircraft in self-defence. The application of this doctrine depends on the circumstances at any given time, but it is clearly exceptional.

(II) NO FLY ZONES (NFZs)

8. The No Fly Zones over Northern and Southern Iraq are not established by UN Security Council Resolutions. They were established in 1991 and 1992 on the basis that they were necessary and proportionate steps were taken to prevent a humanitarian crisis. Prior to the establishment of the Northern No Fly Zone the Security Council had adopted resolution 688 (1991) on 5 April 1991 in which the Council stated that it was gravely concerned by the repression of the Iraqi civilian population in many parts of Iraq, including most recently in Kurdish populated areas, which had led to a massive refugee flow and that it was deeply disturbed by the magnitude of the human suffering involved. The resolution condemned that repression of the Iraqi civilian population and demanded that Iraq immediately end the repression. In our view the purpose of the No Fly Zones is to monitor Iraqi compliance with the provisions of resolution 688. UK and US aircraft patrolling the No Fly Zones are entitled to use force in self-defence where such a use of force is a necessary and proportionate response to actual or imminent attack from Iraqi ground systems.

9. The United States have on occasion claimed that the purpose of the No Fly Zones is to enforce Iraqi compliance with resolutions 687 or 688. This view is not consistent with resolution 687, which does not deal with the repression of the Iraqi population, or with resolution 688, which was not adopted under Chapter VII of the UN Charter and does not contain any provision for enforcement. Nor (as it is sometimes claimed) were the current No Fly Zones provided for in the Safwan agreement, a provisional agreement between coalition and Iraqi commanders of 3 March 1991, laying down military conditions for the cease fire which did not contain any reference to the No Fly Zones.

(III) SECURITY COUNCIL RESOLUTIONS RELEVANT TO THE SANCTIONS REGIME

10. The sanctions regime against Iraq was established by resolutions 661 (1990) of 8 August 1990, which, following the invasion of Kuwait by Iraq, decides that all states shall prevent the import into their territories of any commodities originating in Iraq, the sale or supply to Iraq of any commodities other than medical supplies, and, in

humanitarian circumstances, food stuffs, and that Iraqi funds and financial resources should be frozen. Resolution 661 remains in force. The major exception to the sanctions regime is the oil for food programme which was established by resolution 986 (1993) by Iraq on condition that the purchase price is paid into an escrow account established by the UN Secretary-General, and the funds to that account are used to meet the humanitarian needs of the Iraqi people through the export of medicine, health supplies, foodstuffs and materials and supplies for essential civilian needs. The escrow account is also used to fund the United Nations Compensation Commission and to meet the operating costs of the UN, including those of the United Nations Monitoring, Verification and Inspection Commission (UNMOVIC, see below).

11. The oil for food programme is renewed by the Security Council at (usually) 6 monthly intervals, most recently by resolution 1382 (211) of 29 November 2001. Under that resolution the Council also decided that it would adopt, by 13 May 2002, procedures which would improve the flow of goods to Iraq, other than arms and other potential dual use goods, on a Goods Review List. The United States is currently reviewing the final details of the list with the Russians.

12. In resolution 687 (1991) the Council decided that the prohibition against the import of goods from Iraq should have no further force when Iraq has completed all the actions contemplated in paragraphs 8-13 of that resolution concerning Iraq's weapons of mass destruction programme. Iraq has still not complied with this condition. Under paragraph 21 of resolution 687, the Council decided to review the prohibition against the supply of commodities to Iraq every 60 days in the light of the policies and practices of the Iraqi government, including the implementation of all the relevant resolutions of the Council, for the purpose of determining whether to reduce or lift them. These regular reviews are currently suspended as a result of Iraqi non-compliance with the Council's demands.

13. The intention of the Council to act in accordance with resolution 687 on the termination of these prohibitions has been regularly

reaffirmed, including in resolution 1284 (1999). Paragraph 33 of that resolution also contains a complex formula for the suspension of economic sanctions against Iraq for renewable periods of 120 days, if the United Nations Monitoring, Verification and Inspection Commission and the International Atomic Energy Agency report cooperation in all respects by Iraq in fulfilling work programmed with those bodies for a period of 120 days after a reinforced system of monitoring and verification in Iraq becomes fully operational. Iraq has never complied with these conditions.

(IV) SECURITY COUNCIL RESOLUTIONS RELATING TO UNMOVIC

14. The United Nations Monitoring, Verification and Inspection Commission was established under resolution 687 (1991) (the ceasefire resolution). UNMOVIC is to undertake the responsibilities of the former Special Commission under resolution 687 relating to the destruction of Iraqi chemical and biological weapons and ballistic missiles with a range of over 150 kilometres and the on-going monitoring and verification of Iraq's compliance with these obligations. Like the Special Commission, UNMOVIC is to be allowed unconditional access to all Iraqi facilities, equipment and records as well as to Iraqi officials. Under paragraph 7 of resolution 1284 UNMOVIC and the International Atomic Energy Agency were given the responsibility of drawing up a work programme which would include the implementation of a reinforced system of ongoing monitoring and verification and key remaining disarmament tasks to be completed by Iraq, which constitute the governing standard of Iraqi compliance. There are currently no UNMOVIC personnel in Iraq, and the reinforced ongoing monitoring and verification system has not been implemented because of Iraq's refusal to cooperate.

III
Advice to the Prime Minister

Six days later, on 14 March 2002, David Manning, Mr Blair's foreign policy advisor, briefed the Prime Minister on his meetings with Condoleezza Rice, President Bush's National Security Advisor. He also offered the Prime Minister some advice on his upcoming visit to President Bush's ranch in Crawford, Texas.

SECRET – STRICTLY PERSONAL
FROM : DAVID MANNING
DATE: 14 MARCH 2002
CC: JONATHAN POWELL

PRIME MINISTER
YOUR TRIP TO THE US
I had dinner with Condi on Tuesday; and talks and lunch with her National Security Council team on Wednesday (to which Christopher Meyer also came). These were good exchanges, and particularly frank when we were one-on-one at dinner. I attach the records in case you want to glance.

IRAQ
We spent a long time at dinner on Iraq. It is clear that Bush is grateful for your support and has registered that you are getting flak. I said that you would not budge in your support for regime change but you had to manage a press, a Parliament and a public opinion that was very different than anything in the States. And you would not budge either in your insistence that, if we pursued regime change, it must be very carefully done and produce the right result. Failure was not an option.

Condi's enthusiasm for regime change is undimmed. But there were some signs, since we last spoke, of greater awareness of the practical difficulties and political risks. (See the attached piece by Seymour Hersh which Christopher Meyer says gives a pretty accurate picture of the uncertain state of the debate in Washington.)

From what she said, Bush has yet to find the answers to the big questions:
– how to persuade international opinion that military action against

Iraq is necessary and justified;
– what value to put on the exiled Iraqi opposition;
– how to coordinate a US/allied military campaign with internal opposition (assuming there is any);
– what happens on the morning after?

Bush will want to pick your brains. He will also want to hear whether he can expect coalition support. I told Condi that we realised the Administration could go it alone if it chose. But if it wanted company, it would have to take account of the concerns of its potential coalition partners. In particular:
– the United Nations dimension. The issue of the weapons inspectors must be handled in a way that would persuade European and wider opinion that the United States was conscious of the international framework, and the insistence of many countries on the need for a legal base. Renewed refusal by Saddam to accept unfettered inspections would be a powerful argument;
– the paramount importance of tackling Israel/Palestine. Unless we did, we could find ourselves bombing Iraq and losing the Gulf.

YOUR VISIT TO THE RANCH
No doubt we need to keep a sense of perspective. But my talks with Condi convinced me that Bush wants to hear your views on Iraq before taking decisions. He also wants your support. He is still smarting from the comments by other European leaders on his Iraq policy.

This gives you real influence: on the public relations strategy; on the UN and weapons inspections; and on US planning for any military campaign. This could be critically important. I think there is a real risk that the Administration underestimates the difficulties. They may agree that failure isn't an option, but this does not mean that they will avoid it.

Will the Sunni majority really respond to an uprising led by Kurds and Shias? Will Americans really put in enough ground troops to do the job if the Kurdish/Shi'ite stratagem fails? Even if they do will they be willing to take the sort of casualties that the Republican Guard may inflict on them if it turns out to be an urban war, and Iraqi troops don't conveniently collapse in a heap as Richard Perle and others confidently predict? They need to answer these and other tough questions, in a more convincing way than they have so far before concluding that they can do the business.

The talks at the ranch will also give you the chance to push Bush on the Middle East. The Iraq factor means that there may never be a better opportunity to get this Administration to give sustained attention to reviving the Middle East Peace Process.
DAVID MANNING

IV
News from the Embassy

Meanwhile, Christopher Meyer, the United Kingdom's Ambassador to the United States, had been meeting with Paul Wolfowitz, US Deputy Secretary of Defence. He briefed Manning on what was said in a note dated 18 March.

CONFIDENTIAL AND PERSONAL
British Embassy Washington
From the Ambassador Christopher Meyer KCMG
18 March 2002

Sir David Manning KCMG No. 10 Downing Street

1. Paul Wolfowitz, the Deputy Secretary of Defense, came to Sunday lunch on 17 March.

2. On Iraq I opened by sticking very closely to the script that you used with Condi Rice last week. We backed regime change, but the plan had to be clever and failure was not an option. It would be a tough sell for us domestically, and probably tougher elsewhere in Europe. The United States could go it alone if it wanted to. But if it wanted to act with partners, there had to be a strategy for building support for military action against Saddam. I then went through the need to wrong foot Saddam on the inspectors and the United Nations Security Council Resolutions and the critical importance of the Middle East Peace Process as an integral part of the anti-Saddam strategy. If all this could be accomplished skilfully, we were fairly confident that a number of countries would come on board.

3. I said that the United Kingdom was giving serious thought to publishing a paper that would make the case against Saddam. If the United Kingdom were to join with the United States in any operation against Saddam, we would have to be able to take a critical mass of parliamentary and public opinion with us. It was extraordinary how people had forgotten how bad it was.

4. Wolfowitz said that he fully agreed. He took a slightly different position from others in the Administration, who were focussed on Saddam's capacity to develop weapons of mass destruction. The weapons of mass destruction danger was of course crucial to the public case against Saddam, particularly the potential linkage to terrorism. But Wolfowitz thought it indispensable to spell out in detail Saddam's barbarism. This was well documented from what he had done during the occupation of Kuwait, the incursion into Kurdish territory, the assault on the Marsh Arabs, and to his own people. A lot of work had been done on this towards the end of the first Bush administration. Wolfowitz thought that this would go a long way to destroying any notion of moral equivalence between Iraq and Israel. I said that I had been forcefully struck, when addressing university audiences in the United States, how ready students were to gloss over Saddam's crimes and to blame the United States and the United Kingdom for the suffering of the Iraqi people.

5. Wolfowitz said that it was absurd to deny the link between terrorism and Saddam. There might be doubt about the alleged meeting in Prague between Mohammed Atta, the lead hijacker on 9/11, and Iraqi intelligence (did we, he asked, know anything more about this meeting?). But there were other substantiated cases of Saddam giving comfort to terrorists, including someone involved in the first attack on the World Trade Centre (the latest *New Yorker* apparently has a story about links between Saddam and Al Qaeda operating in Kurdistan).

6. I asked for Wolfowitz's take on the struggle inside the Administration between the pro- and anti- Iraqi National Congress lobbies (well documented in Sy Hersh's recent *New Yorker* piece, which I gave you). He said that he found himself between the two sides (but as the conversation developed, it became clear that Wolfowitz was far more pro-INC than not). He said that he was strongly opposed to what some were advocating: a coalition including all outside factions except the Iraqi National Congress (Iraqi National Accord, Kurdistan Democratic Party, Patriotic Union of Kurdistan, Supreme Council of Islamic Revolution In Iraq). This would not work. Hostility towards the Iraqi National Congress was in reality hostility toward Chalabi. It

was true that Chalabi was not the easiest person to work with. But he had a good record in bringing high-grade defectors out of Iraq. The CIA stubbornly refused to recognise this. They unreasonably denigrated the Iraqi National Congress because of their fixation with Chalabi. When I mentioned that the Iraqi National Congress was penetrated by Iraqi intelligence, Wolfowitz commented that this was probably the case with all the opposition groups: it was something we would have to live with. As to the Kurds, it was true that they were living well (another point to be made in any public dossier on Saddam) and that they feared provoking an incursion by Baghdad. But there were good people among the Kurds, including in particular Salih (?) of the Patriotic Union of Kurdistan. Wolfowitz brushed over my reference to the absence of Sunni in the Iraqi National Congress: there was a big difference between Iraqi and Iranian Shia. The former just wanted to be rid of Saddam.

7. Wolfowitz was pretty dismissive of the desirability of a military coup and of the defector generals in the wings. The latter had blood on their hands. The important thing was to try to have Saddam replaced by something like a functioning democracy. Though imperfect, the Kurdish model was not bad. How to achieve this, I asked? Only through a coalition of all the parties was the answer (we did not get into military planning).

V
Advice for Jack Straw

A few days later, on 22 March, the Political Director at the Foreign and Commonwealth Office, Peter Ricketts, set out for the Foreign Secretary, Jack Straw, what he thought he should advise the Prime Minister about Iraq.

CONFIDENTIAL AND PERSONAL

PR.121

FROM: P F RICKETTS
POLITICAL DIRECTOR

DATE: 22 MARCH 2002
CC: PUS
SECRETARY OF STATE

IRAQ: ADVICE FOR THE PRIME MINISTER

1. You invited thoughts for your personal note to the Prime Minister covering the official advice (we have put up a draft minute separately). Here are mine.

2. By sharing Bush's broad objective the Prime Minister can help shape how it is defined, and the approach to achieving it. In the process, he can bring home to Bush some of the realities which will be less evident from Washington. He can help Bush make good decisions by telling him things his own machine probably isn't.

3. By broad support for the objective brings two real problems which need discussing.

4. First, the THREAT. The truth is that what has changed is not the pace of Saddam Hussein's weapons of mass destruction programmes, but our tolerance of them post-11 September. This is not something we need to be defensive about, but attempts to claim otherwise publicly will increase scepticism about our case. I am relieved that you decided to

postpone publication of the unclassified document. My meeting yesterday showed that there is more work to do to ensure that the figures are accurate and consistent with those of the United States. But even the best survey of Iraq's weapons of mass destruction programmes will not show much advance in recent years on the nuclear, missile or chemical weapons/biological weapons fronts: the programmes are extremely worrying but have not, as far as we know, been stepped up.

5. United States scrambling to establish a link between Iraq and Al Qaida is so far frankly unconvincing. To get public and Parliamentary support for military operations, we have to be convincing that:
– the threat is so serious/imminent that it is worth sending our troops to die for;
– it is qualitatively different from the threat posed by other proliferators who are closer to achieving nuclear capability (including Iran).
We can make the case on qualitative difference (only Iraq has attacked a neighbour, used chemical weapons and fired missiles against Israel). The overall strategy needs to include re-doubled efforts to tackle other proliferators, including Iran, in other ways (the UK/French ideas on greater International Atomic Energy Agency activity are helpful here). But we are still left with a problem of bringing public opinion to accept the imminence of a threat from Iraq. This is something the Prime Minister and President need to have a frank discussion about.

6. The second problem is the END STATE. Military operations need clear and compelling military objectives. For Kosovo it was: Serbs out, Kosovars back, peace-keepers in. For Afghanistan, destroying the Taliban and Al Qaida military capability. For Iraq, 'regime change' does not stack up. It sounds like a grudge between Bush and Saddam. Much better, as you have suggested, to make the objective ending the threat to the international community from Iraqi weapons of mass destruction before Saddam uses it or gives it to the terrorists. This is at once easier to justify in terms of international law but also more demanding. Regime change which produced another Sunni General still in charge of an active Iraqi weapons of mass

destruction programme would be a bad outcome (not least because it would be almost impossible to maintain United Nations sanctions on a new leader who came in promising a fresh start). As with the fight against Osama Bin Laden, Bush would do well to de-personalise the objective focus on elimination of weapons of mass destruction, and show that he is serious about UN Inspectors as the first choice means of achieving that (it is win/win for him: either Saddam against all the odds allows Inspectors to operate freely in which case we can further hobble his weapons of mass destruction programmes, or he blocks/hinders, and we are on stronger ground for switching to other methods).

7. Defining the end state in this way, and working through the United Nations, will of course also help maintain a degree of support among the Europeans, and therefore fits with another major message which the Prime Minister will want to get across: the importance of positioning Iraq as a problem for the international community as a whole not just for the United States.
PETER RICKETTS
CONFIDENTIAL AND PERSONAL

VI
Straw Advises Blair

The Foreign Secretary duly wrote to the Prime Minister three days later.

SECRET AND PERSONAL
PM/02/019
PRIME MINISTER

CRAWFORD/IRAQ
1. The rewards from your visit to Crawford will be few. The risks are high, both for you and for the Government. I judge that there is at present no majority inside the Parliamentary Labour Party for any military action against Iraq, (alongside a greater readiness in the Parliamentary Labour Party to surface their concerns). Colleagues know that Saddam and the Iraqi regime are bad. Making that case is easy. But we have a long way to go to convince them as to:
(a) the scale of the threat from Iraq and why this has got worse recently;
(b) what distinguishes the Iraqi threat from that of e.g. Iran and North Korea so as to justify military action;
(c) the justification for any military action in terms of international law; and
(d) whether the consequence of military action really would be a compliant, law abiding replacement government.

2. The whole exercise is made much more difficult to handle as long as conflict between Israel and the Palestinians is so acute.

THE SCALE OF THE THREAT
3. The Iraqi regime plainly poses a most serious threat to its neighbours, and therefore to international security. However, in the documents so far presented it has been hard to glean whether the threat from Iraq is so significantly different from that of Iran and North Korea as to justify military action (see below).

WHAT IS WORSE NOW?
4. If 11 September had not happened, it is doubtful that the US would now be considering military action against Iraq. In addition, there has

been no credible evidence to link Iraq with Osama Bin Laden and Al Qaida. Objectively, the threat from Iraq has not worsened as a result of 11 September. What has however changed is the tolerance of the international community (especially that of the United States), the world having witnesses on September 11 just what determined evil people can these days perpetuate.

THE DIFFERENCE BETWEEN IRAQ, IRAN AND NORTH KOREA
5. By linking these countries together in this 'axis of evil' speech, President Bush implied an identity between them not only in terms of their threat, but also in terms of the action necessary to deal with the threat. A lot of work will now need to be done to delink the three, and to show why military action against Iraq is so much more justified than against Iran and North Korea. The heart of this case, that Iraq poses a unique and present danger, rests on the facts that it:
- invaded a neighbour;
- has used weapons of mass destruction and would use them again;
- is in breach of nine United Nations Security Council Resolutions.

THE POSITION IN INTERNATIONAL LAW
6. That Iraq is in flagrant breach of international legal obligations imposed on it by the United Nations Security Council provides us with the core of a strategy, and one which is based on international law. Indeed, if the argument is to be won, the whole case against Iraq and in favour (if necessary) of military action, needs to be narrated with reference to the international rule of law.

7. We also have better to sequence the explanation of what we are doing and why. Specifically, we need to concentrate in the early stages on:
- making operational the sanctions regime foreshadowed by UN Security Council Resolution 1382;
- demanding the readmission of weapons inspectors, but this time to operate in a free and unfettered way (a similar formula to that which Cheney used at your joint press conference, as I recall).

8. I know there are those who say that an attack on Iraq would be justified whether or not weapons inspectors were readmitted. But I

believe that a demand for the unfettered readmission of weapons inspectors is essential, in terms of public explanation, and in terms of legal sanction for any subsequent military action.

9. Legally there are two potential elephant traps:
(i) regime change per se is no justification for military action; it could form part of the method of any strategy, but not a goal. Of course, we may want credibly to assert that regime change is an essential part of the strategy by which we have to achieve our ends – that of the elimination of Iraq's weapons of mass destruction capacity; but the latter has to be the goal;
(ii) on whether any military action would require a fresh United Nations Security Council mandate (Desert Fox did not). The United States is likely to oppose any idea of a fresh mandate. On the other side, the weight of legal advice here is that a fresh mandate may well be required. There is no doubt that a new United Nations Security Council Resolution would transform the climate in the Parliamentary Labour Party. Whilst that (a new mandate) is very unlikely, given the United States' position, a draft resolution against military action with 13 in favour (or handsitting) and two vetoes against could play very badly here.

THE CONSEQUENCES OF ANY MILITARY ACTION
10. A legal justification is a necessary but far from sufficient pre-condition for military action. We have also to answer the big question – what will this action achieve? There seems to be a larger hole in this than on anything. Most of the assessments from the United States have assumed regime change as a means of eliminating Iraq's weapons of mass destruction threat. But none have satisfactorily answered how that regime change is to be secured, and how there can be any certainty that the replacement regime will be better.

11. Iraq has had NO history of democracy so no one has this habit or experience.

(JACK STRAW)
Foreign and Commonwealth Office
25 March 2002
SECRET AND PERSONAL

VII
Countdown

Four months later, there was still considerable uncertainty about how to present Britain's role in relation to US plans for the coming war. The Cabinet Office, in a note dated 21 July 2002, briefed participants at the meeting of Blair's inner circle, which was to be held on 23 July. The paper is incomplete because the last page is missing. The minutes of the 23 July meeting (see below), when they were leaked almost three years later, on 1 May 2005, became known as the 'Downing Street Memo'.

PERSONAL SECRET UK EYES ONLY

IRAQ: CONDITIONS FOR MILITARY ACTION (A Note by Officials)

Summary

Ministers are invited to:
(1) Note the latest position on United States military planning and timescales for possible action.

(2) Agree that the objective of any military action should be a stable and law-abiding Iraq, within present borders, co-operating with the international community, no longer posing a threat to its neighbours or international security, and abiding by its international obligations on weapons of mass destruction.

(3) Agree to engage the United States on the need to set military plans within a realistic political strategy, which includes identifying the succession to Saddam Hussein and creating the conditions necessary to justify government military action, which might include an ultimatum for the return of United Nations weapons inspectors to Iraq. This should include a call from the Prime Minister to President Bush ahead of the briefing of United States military plans to the President on 4 August.

(4) Note the potentially long lead times involved in equipping United

Kingdom Armed Forces to undertake operations in the Iraqi theatre and agree that the Ministry Of Defence should bring forward proposals for the procurement of Urgent Operational Requirements under cover of the lessons learned from Afghanistan and the outcome of the Spending Review 2002.

(5) Agree to the establishment of an ad hoc group of officials under Cabinet Office Chairmanship to consider the development of an information campaign to be agreed with the United States.

INTRODUCTION
1. The United States Government's military planning for action against Iraq is proceeding apace. But, as yet, it lacks a political framework. In particular, little thought has been given to creating the political conditions for military action, or the aftermath and how to shape it.

2. When the Prime Minister discussed Iraq with President Bush at Crawford in April he said that the United Kingdom would support military action to bring about regime change, provided that certain conditions were met: efforts had been made to construct a coalition/shape public opinion, the Israel-Palestine Crisis was quiescent, and the options for action to eliminate Iraq's weapons of mass destruction through the UN weapons inspectors had been exhausted.

3. We need now to reinforce this message and to encourage the United States Government to place its military planning within a political framework, partly to forestall the risk that military action is precipitated in an unplanned way by, for example, an incident in the No Fly Zones. This is particularly important for the United Kingdom because it is necessary to create the conditions in which we could legally support military action. Otherwise we face the real danger that the United States will commit themselves to a course of action which we would find very difficult to support.

4. In order to fulfil the conditions set out by the Prime Minister for United Kingdom support for military action against Iraq, certain

preparations need to be made, and other considerations taken into account. This note sets them out in a form which can be adapted for use with the United States Government. Depending on US intentions, a decision in principle may be needed soon on whether and in what form the United Kingdom takes part in military action.

THE GOAL
5. Our objective should be a stable and law-abiding Iraq, within present borders, co-operating with the international community, no longer posing a threat to its neighbours or to international security, and abiding by its international obligations on weapons of mass destruction. It seems unlikely that this could be achieved while the current Iraqi regime remains in power. US military planning unambiguously takes as its objective the removal of Saddam Hussein's regime, followed by elimination if Iraqi weapons of mass destruction. It is however, by no means certain, in the view of United Kingdom officials, that one would necessarily follow from the other. Even if regime change is a necessary condition for controlling Iraqi weapons of mass destruction, it is certainly not a sufficient one.

US MILITARY PLANNING
6. Although no political decisions have been taken, US military planners have drafted options for the United States Government to undertake an invasion of Iraq. In a 'Running Start', military action could begin as early as November of this year, with no overt military build-up. Air strikes and support for opposition groups in Iraq would lead initially to small-scale land operations, with further land forces deploying sequentially, ultimately overwhelming Iraqi forces and leading to the collapse of the Iraqi regime. A 'Generated Start' would involve a longer build-up before any military action were taken, as early as January 2003. US military plans include no specifics on the strategic context either before or after the campaign. Currently the preference appears to be for the 'Running Start'. The Chief of Defence Staff will be ready to brief Ministers in more detail.

7. United States plans assume, as a minimum, the use of British bases in Cyprus and Diego Garcia. This means that legal base issues would

arise virtually whatever option Ministers choose with regard to United Kingdom participation.

THE VIABILITY OF THE PLANS
8. The Chiefs of Staff have discussed the viability of US military plans. Their initial view is that there are a number of questions which would have to be answered before they could assess whether the plans are sound. Notably these include the realism of the 'Running Start', the extent to which the plans are proof against Iraqi counter-attack using chemical or biological weapons and the robustness of United States assumptions about the bases and about Iraqi (un)willingness to fight.

UK MILITARY CONTRIBUTION
9. The United Kingdom's ability to contribute forces depends on the details of the US military planning and the time available to prepare and deploy them. The Ministry Of Defence is examining how the United Kingdom might contribute to US-led action. The options range from deployment of a Division (i.e. Gulf War sized contribution plus naval and air forces) to making available bases. It is already clear that the United Kingdom could not generate a Division in time for an operation in January 2003, unless publicly visible decisions were taken very soon. Maritime and air forces could be deployed in time, provided adequate basing arrangements could be made. The lead times involved in preparing for United Kingdom military involvement include the procurement of Urgent Operational Requirements, for which there is no financial provision.

THE CONDITIONS NECESSARY FOR MILITARY ACTION
10. Aside from the existence of a viable military plan we consider the following conditions necessary for military action and United Kingdom participation: justification/legal base; an international coalition; a quiescent Israel/Palestine; a positive risk/benefit assessment; and the preparation of domestic opinion.

JUSTIFICATION
11. The United States views of international law vary from that of the United Kingdom and the international community. Regime change

per se is not a proper basis for military action under international law. But regime change could result from action that is otherwise lawful. We would regard the use of force against Iraq, or any other state, as lawful if exercised in the right of individual or collective self-defence, if carried out to avert an overwhelming humanitarian catastrophe, or authorised by the UN Security Council. A detailed consideration of the legal issues, prepared earlier this year, is at Annex A. The legal position would depend on the precise circumstances at the time. Legal bases for an invasion of Iraq are in principle conceivable in both the first two instances but would be difficult to establish because of, for example, the tests of immediacy and proportionality. Further legal advice would be needed on this point.

12. This leaves the route under the United Nations Security Council resolutions on weapons inspectors. Kofi Annan has held three rounds of meetings with Iraq in an attempt to persuade them to admit the UN weapons inspectors. These have made no substantive progress; the Iraqis are deliberately obfuscating. Annan has downgraded the dialogue but more pointless talks are possible. We need to persuade the United Nations and the international community that this situation cannot be allowed to continue *ad infinitum*. We need to set a deadline, leading to an ultimatum. It would be preferable to obtain backing of a United Nations Security Council Resolution for any ultimatum and early work would be necessary to explore with Kofi Annan and the Russians, in particular, the scope for achieving this.

13. In practice, facing pressure of military action, Saddam is likely to admit weapons inspectors as a means of forestalling it. But once admitted, he would not allow them to operate freely. UNMOVIC (the successor to UNSCOM) will take at least six months after entering Iraq to establish the monitoring and verification system under Resolution 1284 necessary to assess whether Iraq is meeting its obligations. Hence, even if United Nations inspectors gained access today, by January 2003 they would at best only just be completing setting up. It is possible that they will encounter Iraqi obstruction during this period, but this is more likely when they are fully operational.

14. It is just possible that an ultimatum could be cast in terms which Saddam would reject (because he is unwilling to accept unfettered access) and which would not be regarded as unreasonable by the international community. However, failing that (or an Iraqi attack) we would be most unlikely to achieve a legal base for military action by January 2003.

AN INTERNATIONAL COALITION
15. An international coalition is necessary to provide a military platform and desirable for political purposes.

16. US military planning assumes that the United States would be allowed to use bases in Kuwait (air and ground forces), Jordan, in the Gulf (air and naval forces) and UK territory (Diego Garcia and our bases in Cyprus). The plans assume that Saudi Arabia would withhold co-operation except granting military over-flights. On the assumption that military action would involve operations in the Kurdish area in the North of Iraq, the use of bases in Turkey would also be necessary.

17. In the absence of United Nations authorisation, there will be problems in securing the support of NATO and European Union partners. Australia would be likely to participate on the same basis as the United Kingdom. France might be prepared to take part if she saw military action as inevitable. Russia and China, seeking to improve their United States relations, might set aside their misgivings if sufficient attention were paid to their legal and economic concerns. Probably the best we could expect from the region would be neutrality. The United States is likely to restrain Israel from taking part in military action. In practice, much of the international community would find it difficult to stand in the way of the determined course of the US hegemon. However, the greater the international support, the greater the prospects of success.

A QUIESCENT ISRAEL-PALESTINE
18. The Israeli re-occupation of the West Bank has dampened Palestinian violence for the time being but is unsustainable in the long-term and stoking more trouble for the future. The Bush speech

was at best a half step forward. We are using the Palestinian reform agenda to make progress, including a resumption of political negotiations. The Americans are talking of a ministerial conference in November or later. Real progress towards a viable Palestinian state is the best way to undercut Palestinian extremists and reduce Arab antipathy to military action against Saddam Hussein. However, another upsurge of Palestinian/Israeli violence is highly likely. The co-incidence of such an upsurge with the preparations for military action against Iraq cannot be ruled out. Indeed Saddam would use continuing violence in the Occupied Territories to bolster popular Arab support for his regime.

BENEFITS/RISKS
19. Even with a legal base and a viable military plan, we would still need to ensure that the benefits of action outweigh the risks. In particular, we need to be sure that the outcome of the military action would match our objective as set out in paragraph 5 above. A post-war occupation of Iraq could lead to a protracted and costly nation-building exercise. As already made clear, the US military plans are virtually silent on this point. Washington could look to us to share a disproportionate share of the burden. Further work is required to define more precisely the means by which the desired endstate would be created, in particular what form of Government might replace Saddam Hussein's regime and the timescale within which it would be possible to identify a successor. We must also consider in greater detail the impact of military action on other United Kingdom interests in the region.

DOMESTIC OPINION
20. Time will be required to prepare public opinion in the United Kingdom that it is necessary to take military action against Saddam Hussein. There would also need to be a substantial effort to secure the support of Parliament. An information campaign will be needed which has to be closely related to an overseas information campaign designed to influence Saddam Hussein, the Islamic World and the wider international community. This will need to give full coverage to the threat posed by Saddam Hussein, including his weapons of mass destruction, and the legal justification for action.

TIMESCALES

21. Although the US military could act against Iraq as soon as November, we judge that a military campaign is unlikely to start until January 2003, if only because of the time it will take to reach consensus in Washington. That said, we judge that for climatic reasons, military action would need to start by January 2003, unless action were deferred until the following autumn.

22. As this paper makes clear, even this timescale would present problems. This means that:
(a) We need to influence United States consideration of the military plans before President Bush is briefed on 4 August, through contacts between the Prime Minister and the President and at other levels;

The final page of this memo is missing.

VIII
The Downing Street Memo

This revealing memorandum about the United Kingdom's position and preparations for war on Iraq, dating from July 2002, was leaked to the press in the days before the General Election. It speaks for itself and we reprint it in full.

SECRET AND STRICTLY PERSONAL – UK EYES ONLY
To: DAVID MANNING
From: Matthew Rycroft
Date: 23 July 2002
S 195 /02

cc: Defence Secretary, Foreign Secretary, Attorney-General, Sir Richard Wilson, John Scarlett, Francis Richards, CDS [Chief of Defence Staff], C [Head of the Secret Intelligence Service], Jonathan Powell, Sally Morgan, Alastair Campbell

IRAQ: PRIME MINISTER'S MEETING, 23 JULY
Copy addressees and you met the Prime Minister on 23 July to discuss Iraq.
This record is extremely sensitive. No further copies should be made. It should be shown only to those with a genuine need to know its contents.

John Scarlett summarised the intelligence and latest Joint Intelligence Committee (JIC) assessment. Saddam's regime was tough and based on extreme fear. The only way to overthrow it was likely to be by massive military action. Saddam was worried and expected an attack, probably by air and land, but he was not convinced that it would be immediate or overwhelming. His regime expected their neighbours to line up with the US. Saddam knew that regular army morale was poor. Real support for Saddam among the public was probably narrowly based.

C reported on his recent talks in Washington. There was a perceptible shift in attitude. Military action was now seen as inevitable. Bush wanted to remove Saddam, through military action, justified by the conjunction of terrorism and weapons of mass destruction

The Dodgiest Dossier

(WMD). But the intelligence and facts were being fixed around the policy. The National Security Council (NSC) had no patience with the UN route, and no enthusiasm for publishing material on the Iraqi regime's record. There was little discussion in Washington of the aftermath after military action.

The Chief of Defence Staff (CDS) said that military planners would brief US Central Command (CENTCOM) on 1-2 August, Rumsfeld on 3 August and Bush on 4 August.

The two broad US options were:

(a) Generated Start. A slow build-up of 250,000 US troops, a short (72 hour) air campaign, then a move up to Baghdad from the south. Lead time of 90 days (30 days preparation plus 60 days deployment to Kuwait).

(b) Running Start. Use forces already in theatre (3 x 6,000), continuous air campaign, initiated by an Iraqi *casus belli*. Total lead time of 60 days with the air campaign beginning even earlier. A hazardous option.

The US saw the UK (and Kuwait) as essential, with basing in Diego Garcia and Cyprus critical for either option. Turkey and other Gulf states were also important, but less vital. The three main options for UK involvement were:

(i) Basing in Diego Garcia and Cyprus, plus three Special Forces (SF) squadrons.

(ii) As above, with maritime and air assets in addition.

(iii) As above, plus a land contribution of up to 40,000, perhaps with a discrete role in Northern Iraq entering from Turkey, tying down two Iraqi divisions.

The Defence Secretary said that the US had already begun 'spikes of activity' to put pressure on the regime. No decisions had been taken, but he thought the most likely timing in US minds for military action to begin was January, with the timeline beginning 30 days before the US Congressional elections.

The Foreign Secretary said he would discuss this with Colin Powell this week. It seemed clear that Bush had made up his mind to take military action, even if the timing was not yet decided. But the case was thin. Saddam was not threatening his neighbours, and his WMD capability was less than that of Libya, North Korea or Iran. We should work up a plan for an ultimatum to Saddam to allow back in the UN weapons inspectors. This would also help with the legal justification for the use of force.

The Attorney-General said that the desire for regime change was not a legal base for military action. There were three possible legal bases: self-defence, humanitarian intervention, or United Nations Security Council (UNSC) authorisation. The first and second could not be the base in this case. Relying on UNSCR 1205 of three years ago would be difficult. The situation might of course change.

The Prime Minister said that it would make a big difference politically and legally if Saddam refused to allow in the UN inspectors. Regime change and weapons of mass destruction were linked in the sense that it was the regime that was producing the weapons of mass destruction. There were different strategies for dealing with Libya and Iran. If the political context were right, people would support regime change. The two key issues were whether the military plan worked and whether we had the political strategy to give the military plan the space to work.

On the first, the Chief of Defence Staff said that we did not know yet if the US battleplan was workable. The military were continuing to ask lots of questions.

For instance, what were the consequences, if Saddam used weapons of mass destruction on day one, or if Baghdad did not collapse and urban warfighting began? You said that Saddam could also use his weapons of mass destruction on Kuwait. Or on Israel, added the Defence Secretary.

The Foreign Secretary thought the US would not go ahead with a military plan unless convinced that it was a winning strategy. On this, US and UK interests converged. But on the political strategy, there could be US/UK differences. Despite US resistance, we should explore discreetly the ultimatum. Saddam would continue to play hard-ball with the UN.

John Scarlett assessed that Saddam would allow the inspectors back in only when he thought the threat of military action was real.

The Defence Secretary said that if the Prime Minister wanted UK military involvement, he would need to decide this early. He cautioned that many in the US did not think it worth going down the ultimatum route. It would be important for the Prime Minister to set out the political context to Bush.

CONCLUSIONS:
(a) We should work on the assumption that the UK would take part in any military action. But we needed a fuller picture of US planning before we could take any firm decisions. The Chief of Defence Staff should tell the US military that we were considering a range of options.
(b) The Prime Minister would revert on the question of whether funds could be spent in preparation for this operation.
(c) The Chief of Defence Staff would send the Prime Minister full details of the proposed military campaign and possible UK contributions by the end of the week.
(d) The Foreign Secretary would send the Prime Minister the background on the UN inspectors, and discreetly work up the ultimatum to Saddam. He would also send the Prime Minister advice on the positions of countries in the region especially Turkey, and of the key EU member states.
(e) John Scarlett would send the Prime Minister a full intelligence update.
(f) We must not ignore the legal issues: the Attorney-General would consider legal advice with Foreign and Commonwealth Office/Ministry of Defence legal advisers.
(I have written separately to commission this follow-up work.)
MATTHEW RYCROFT
[Rycroft was a Downing Street foreign policy aide]

IX
An Early Start to the Air War

The war on Iraq was already some ten months old by the time the land assault began in March 2003. From May 2002, two months before the meeting that gave rise to the Downing Street Memo's reference by Defence Secretary Hoon to 'spikes of activity', the US Air Force and the RAF had increased aerial bombardment, attacking targets under cover of patrolling the no-fly zones in northern and southern Iraq. This commentary was prepared by Tony Simpson.

The United Kingdom and United States air forces patrolled the northern and southern No Fly Zones which were established in Iraq from 1991 and 1992 respectively. These zones never received any United Nations endorsement. The Foreign Office states that British aircraft were authorised to fire in self-defence. When asked about this in the House of Commons on 17 June 2002, Defence Secretary Hoon replied:

> 'The air strikes are self-defence against attacks on our aircraft and on coalition aircraft patrolling the no-fly zone, so their primary purpose is to defend aircrew and their aircraft against those attacks. The humanitarian purpose of having planes patrolling the no-fly zone continues.'

Mike O'Brien, then a Foreign Office Minister, repeated this line in a Commons written answer dated 10 December 2002:

> 'Since late 1998, Iraq has waged a systematic campaign to shoot down allied aircraft patrolling the no-fly zones. This is contrary to international law and inconsistent with UN resolutions. We only take action to protect our aircrew. UK and US pilots are authorised to respond to Iraqi attack in self-defence.'

Geoff Hoon elaborated the same line, also in a written answer dated 16 January 2003, just two months before the start of the ground war:

> 'Coalition aircrew only ever respond in self-defence against military targets. When attacks by Iraqi air defences force coalition aircraft to respond in this way, we go to great lengths to ensure that the risk of civilian casualties is minimised. Targets are selected with extreme care and precision-guided weapons are used.'

He repeated this line, and denied any liability for compensation, on 21 January 2003:

> 'Coalition aircraft monitoring the no fly zones over Iraq respond in self-defence only to the sustained efforts of Iraq's defences to shoot them down. They do so, in accordance with international law, only against targets posing a threat to the safety of our forces. No liability to pay compensation arises.'

Then, on 3 March 2003, days before the start of the ground war, Hoon told the House of Commons:

> 'I emphasise to the House that no decision has been taken about the use of military force, and I repeat that there is no substantial change in the operation of the northern or southern no-fly zones.'

Yet, in December 2002, the Ministry of Defence gave figures to Sir Menzies Campbell, the Liberal Democrat spokesman on Foreign Affairs, that showed that ordnance dropped on southern Iraq had increased by 300% since March that year. The total tonnage of ordnance released over Iraq between March 1 and November 13 2002 was 126.4 tonnes. This is an average of nearly 15 tonnes a month — a 60% increase over the preceding year. Ordnance weighing 0.3 tonnes was dropped in April, a figure which rose dramatically to more than 54 tonnes in September.

Sir Menzies Campbell commented at the time:

> 'The inference is that these operations have little to do with humanitarian purposes but are being carried out to soften up Iraq air defence systems. There must be a risk that escalation of this kind could provoke wider military action at a time when the inspectors still appear to be able to carry out their work.'

On 4 December 2002, Richard Norton-Taylor writing in *The Guardian* reported that

> 'Last month Britain and America stepped up the hidden air war over Iraq, with RAF fighters based in Saudi Arabia supporting US navy attack aircraft in practice bombing runs on Iraqi targets. US navy Super Hornets from the aircraft carrier Abraham Lincoln, which is in the Gulf, carried out mock attacks on airfields, control towers, and other military sites. *The New*

York Times reported American commanders as saying that the aircraft were "acquainting themselves" with targets they may be called on to attack and were being supported by RAF aircraft. Earlier this week, Iraqi officials said four people had been killed by western warplanes.'

The Downing Street memo of 23 July records Defence Secretary Hoon as saying that 'the US had already begun "spikes of activity" to put pressure on the regime.' This was illegal under international law, according to the leaked Foreign Office legal advice first provided to senior ministers in March 2002 (see II above). Yet, two months later, RAF and USAF jets began the 'spikes of activity' which might goad Saddam Hussein into retaliating and give the allies a pretext for war, as Michael Smith pointed out in *The Los Angeles Times* (23 June 2005).

The Foreign Office advice shows military action to pressurise the regime was 'not consistent with' UN law, despite American claims that it was. It said that allied aircraft were legally entitled to patrol the no-fly zones over the north and south of Iraq only to deter attacks by Saddam's forces on the Kurdish and Shia populations. The allies had no power to use military force to put pressure of any kind on the regime.

The increased attacks on Iraqi installations, which senior US officers admitted were designed to 'degrade' Iraqi air defences, began six months before the UN passed resolution 1441, which the allies claim authorised military action.

The Foreign Office advice noted that the Americans had 'on occasion' claimed that the allied aircraft were there to enforce compliance with resolutions 688 and 687, which ordered Iraq to destroy its weapons of mass destruction. 'This view is not consistent with resolution 687, which does not deal with the repression of the Iraqi civilian population, or with resolution 688, which was not adopted under Chapter VII of the UN Charter, and does not contain any provision for enforcement,' it said.

Further intensification of the bombing, known in the Pentagon as the Blue Plan, began at the end of August, 2002, following a meeting of the US National Security Council at the White House that month. As Michael Smith wrote in the *Sunday Times* on 19 June 2005, 'General Tommy Franks, the allied commander, recalled in his autobiography, *American Soldier*, that during this meeting he rejected a call from

The Dodgiest Dossier

Condoleezza Rice, the national security adviser, to cut the bombing patrols because he wanted to use them to make Iraq's defences "as weak as possible". The allied commander specifically used the term "spikes of activity" in his book.'

The story of the early start to the air war was developed in the next edition of the *Sunday Times* (26 June 2005), when Michael Smith wrote under the headline 'General admits to secret air war':

> 'The American general who commanded allied air forces during the Iraq war appears to have admitted in a briefing to American and British officers that coalition aircraft waged a secret air war against Iraq from the middle of 2002, nine months before the invasion began. Addressing a briefing on lessons learnt from the Iraq war Lieutenant-General Michael Moseley said that in 2002 and early 2003 allied aircraft flew 21,736 sorties, dropping more than 600 bombs on 391 'carefully selected targets' before the war officially started. The nine months of allied raids 'laid the foundations' for the allied victory, Moseley said. They ensured that allied forces did not have to start the war with a protracted bombardment of Iraqi positions... Moseley told the briefing at Nellis airbase in Nebraska on 17 July 2003, that the raids took place under cover of patrols of the southern no-fly zone; their purpose was ostensibly to protect the ethnic minorities.'

X
The Attorney General's Advice

On 7 March 2003, when it was apparent that there would be no second UN Security Council resolution authorising the use of force against Iraq, the Attorney General, Peter Goldsmith, responded to a request from the Prime Minister for advice on the legality of military action in those circulmstances.

SECRET

ATTORNEY GENERAL

PRIME MINISTER

IRAQ: RESOLUTION 1441

1. You have asked me for advice on the legality of military action against Iraq without a further resolution of the Security Council. This is, of course, a matter we have discussed before. Since then I have had the benefit of discussions with the Foreign Secretary and Sir Jeremy Greenstock, who have given me valuable background information on the negotiating history of resolution 1441. In addition, I have also had the opportunity to hear the views of the US Administration from their perspective as co-sponsors of the resolution.

This note considers the issues in detail in order that you are in a position to understand the legal reasoning. My conclusions are summarised at paragraphs 26 to 31 below.

POSSIBLE LEGAL BASES FOR THE USE OF FORCE

2. As I have previously advised, there are generally three possible bases for the use of force:
(a) self-defence (which may include collective self-defence);
(b) exceptionally, to avert overwhelming humanitarian catastrophe; and
(c) authorisation by the Security Council acting under Chapter VII of the UN Charter.

3. Force may be used in **self-defence** if there is an actual or imminent threat of an armed attack; the use of force must be necessary, i.e. the only means of averting an attack; and the force used must be a

proportionate response. It is now widely accepted that an imminent armed attack will justify the use of force if the other conditions are met. The concept of what is imminent may depend on the circumstances. Different considerations may apply, for example, where the risk is of attack from terrorists sponsored or harboured by a particular State, or where there is a threat of an attack by nuclear weapons. However, in my opinion there must be some degree of imminence. I am aware that the USA has been arguing for recognition of a broad doctrine of a right to use force to pre-empt danger in the future. If this means more than a right to respond proportionately to an imminent attack (and I understand that the doctrine is intended to carry that connotation) this is not a doctrine which, in my opinion, exists or is recognised in international law.

4. The use of force to avert **overwhelming humanitarian catastrophe** has been emerging as a further, and exceptional, basis for the use of force. It was relied on by the United Kingdom in the Kosovo crisis and is the underlying justification for the No-Fly Zones. The doctrine remains controversial, however. I know of no reason why it would be an appropriate basis for action in present circumstances.

5. Force may be used where this is **authorised by the UN Security Council** acting under Chapter VII of the UN Charter. The key question is whether resolution 1441 has the effect of providing such authorisation.

RESOLUTION 1441

6. As you are aware, the argument that resolution 1441 itself provides the authorisation to use force depends on the revival of the express authorisation to use force given in 1990 by Security Council resolution 678. This in turn gives rise to two questions:
(a) is the so-called 'revival argument' a sound legal basis in principle?
(b) is resolution 1441 sufficient to revive the authorisation in resolution 678?

I deal with these questions in turn. It is a trite, but nonetheless relevant observation given what some commentators have been saying, that if the answer to these two questions is 'yes', the use of force will have been authorised by the United Nations and not in defiance of it.

THE REVIVAL ARGUMENT

7. Following its invasion and annexation of Kuwait, the Security Council authorised the use of force against Iraq in resolution 678 (1990). This resolution authorised coalition forces to use all necessary means to force Iraq to withdraw from Kuwait and to restore international peace and security in the area. The resolution gave a legal basis for Operation Desert Storm, which was brought to an end by the cease-fire set out by the Council in resolution 687 (1991). The conditions for the cease-fire in that resolution (and subsequent resolutions) imposed obligations on Iraq with regard to the elimination of weapons of mass destruction and monitoring of its obligations. Resolution 687 suspended, but did not terminate, the authority to use force in resolution 678. Nor has any subsequent resolution terminated the authorisation to use force in resolution 678. It has been the United Kingdom's view that a violation of Iraq's obligations under resolution 687 which is sufficiently serious to undermine the basis of the cease-fire can revive the authorisation to use force in resolution 678.

8. In reliance on this argument, force has been used on certain occasions. I am advised by the Foreign Office Legal Advisers that this was the basis for the use of force between 13 and 18 January 1993 following United Nations Presidential Statements on 8 and 11 January 1993 condemning particular failures by Iraq to observe the terms of the cease-fire resolution. The revival argument was also the basis for the use of force in December 1998 by the United States and United Kingdom (Operation Desert Fox). This followed a series of Security Council resolutions, notably, resolution 1205 (1998).

9. Law Officers have advised in the past that, provided the conditions are made out, the revival argument does provide a sufficient justification in international law for the use of force against Iraq. That view is supported by an opinion given in August 1992 by the then United Nations Legal Counsel, Carl-August Fleischauer. However, the United Kingdom has consistently taken the view (as did the

Fleischauer opinion) that, as the cease-fire conditions were set by the Security Council in resolution 687, it is for the Council to assess whether any such breach of those obligations has occurred. The United States have a rather different view: they maintain that the fact of whether Iraq is in breach is a matter of objective fact which may therefore be assessed by individual Member States. I am not aware of any other state which supports this view. This is an issue of critical importance when considering the effect of resolution 1441.

10. The revival argument is controversial. It is not widely accepted among academic commentators. However, I agree with my predecessors' advice on this issue. Further, I believe that the arguments in support of the revival argument are stronger following adoption of resolution 1441. That is because of the terms of the resolution and the course of the negotiations which led to its adoption. Thus, preambular paragraphs 4, 5 and 10 recall the authorisation to use force in resolution 678 and that resolution 687 imposed obligations on Iraq as a necessary condition of the cease-fire. Operative paragraph (OP)1 provides that Iraq has been and remains in material breach of its obligations under relevant resolutions, including the resolution 687. Operative paragraph 13 recalls that Iraq has been warned repeatedly that 'serious consequences' will result from continued violations of its obligations. The previous practice of the Council and statements made by Council members during the negotiation of resolution 1441 demonstrate that the phrase 'material breach' signifies a finding by the Council of a sufficiently serious breach of the cease-fire conditions to revive the authorisation in resolution 678 and that 'serious consequences' is accepted as indicating the use of force.

11. I disagree, therefore, with those commentators and lawyers, who assert that nothing less than an explicit authorisation to use force in a Security Council resolution will be sufficient.

SUFFICIENCY OF RESOLUTION 1441

12. In order for the authorisation to use force in resolution 678 to be revived, there needs to be a determination by the Security Council that there is a violation of the conditions of the cease-fire and that the Security Council considers it sufficiently serious to destroy the basis of

the cease-fire. Revival will not. however, take place, notwithstanding a finding of violation, if the Security Council has made it clear either that action short of the use of force should be taken to ensure compliance with the terms of the cease-fire, or that it intends to decide subsequently what action is required to ensure compliance. Notwithstanding the determination of material breach in operative paragraph 1 of resolution 1441, it is clear that the Council did not intend that the authorisation in resolution 678 should revive immediately following the adoption of resolution 1441, since operative paragraph 2 of the resolution affords Iraq a 'final opportunity' to comply with its disarmament obligations under previous resolutions by cooperating with the enhanced inspection regime described in operative paragraphs 3 and 5-9. But operative paragraph 2 also states that the Council has determined that compliance with resolution 1441 is Iraq's last chance before the cease-fire resolution will be enforced. Operative paragraph 2 has the effect therefore of suspending the legal consequences of the operative paragraph 1 determination of material breach which would otherwise have triggered the revival of the authorisation in resolution 678. The narrow but key question is: on the true interpretation of resolution 1441, what has the Security Council decided will be the consequences of Iraq's failure to comply with the enhanced regime.

13. The provisions relevant to determining whether or not Iraq has taken the final opportunity given by the Security Council are contained in operative paragraphs 4, 11 and 12 of the resolution.
– operative paragraph 4 provides that false statements or omissions in the declaration to be submitted by Iraq under operative paragraph 3 and failure by Iraq at any time to comply with and cooperate fully in the implementation of resolution 1441 will constitute a further material breach of Iraq's obligations and will be reported to the Council for assessment under paragraphs 11 and 12 of the resolution.
– operative paragraph 11 directs the Executive Chairman of UNMOVIC and the Director-General of the International Atomic Energy Agency to report immediately to the Council any interference by Iraq with inspection activities, as well as any failure by Iraq to comply with its disarmament obligations, including the obligations regarding inspections under resolution 1441.

– operative paragraph 12 provides that the Council will convene immediately on receipt of a report in accordance with paragraphs 4 or 11 'in order to consider the situation and the need for compliance with all of the relevant Council resolutions in order to secure international peace and security'.

It is clear from the text of the resolution, and is apparent from the negotiating history, that if Iraq fails to comply, there will be a further Security Council discussion. The text is, however, ambiguous and unclear on what happens next.

14. There are two competing arguments:
(i) that provided there is a Council discussion, if it does not reach a conclusion, there remains an authorisation to use force;
(ii) that nothing short of a further Council decision will be a legitimate basis for the use of force.

THE FIRST ARGUMENT
15. The first argument is based on the following steps:
(a) operative paragraph 1, by stating that Iraq 'has been and remains in material breach' of its obligations under relevant resolutions, including resolution 687 amounts to a determination by the Council that Iraq's violations of resolution 687 are sufficiently serious to destroy the basis of the cease-fire and therefore, in principle, to revive the authorisation to use force in resolution 678;
(b) the Council decided, however, to give Iraq 'a final opportunity' (operative paragraph 2) but because of the clear warning that it faced 'serious consequences as a result of its continued violations' (operative paragraph 13) was warning that a failure to take that 'final opportunity' would lead to such consequences;
(c) further, by operative paragraph 4, the Council decided in advance that false statements or omissions in its declaration and 'failure by Iraq at any time to comply with, and cooperate fully in the implementation of, this resolution' would constitute 'a further material breach'; the argument is that the Council's determination in advance that particular conduct would constitute a material breach (thus reviving the authorisation to use force) is as good as its determination after the event;

(d) in either event, the Council must meet (operative paragraph 12) 'to consider the situation and the need for full compliance with all of the relevant Council resolutions in order to secure international peace and security', but the resolution singularly does not say that the Council must decide what action to take. The Council knew full well, it is argued, the difference between 'consider' and 'decide' and so the omission is highly significant. Indeed, the omission is especially important as the French and Russians made proposals to include an express requirement for a further decision, but these were rejected precisely to avoid being tied to the need to obtain a second resolution. On this view, therefore, while the Council has the opportunity to take a further decision, the determinations of material breach in operative paragraphs 1 and 4 remain valid even if the Council does not act.

THE SECOND ARGUMENT

16. The second argument focuses, by contrast, on two provisions in particular of the resolution: first, the final words in operative paragraph 4 ('and will be reported to the Council for assessment in accordance with paragraphs 11 and 12 below') and, second, the requirement in operative paragraph 12 for the Council to 'consider the situation and the need for full compliance with all of the relevant Council resolutions in order to secure international peace and security'. Taken together, it is argued, these provisions indicate that the Council decided in resolution 1441 that in the event of continued Iraqi non-compliance, the issue should return to the Council for a further decision on what action should be taken at that stage.

DISCUSSION

17. So far as operative paragraph 4 of the resolution is concerned, one view is that the words at the end of this paragraph indicate the need for an assessment by the Security Council of how serious any Iraqi breaches really are and whether they are sufficiently serious to destroy the basis of the cease-fire. This argument is supported by public statements to the effect that only serious cases of non-compliance will constitute a further material breach. Thus, the Foreign Secretary stated in Parliament on 25 November that 'material breach means something significant; some behaviour or pattern of

behaviour that is serious. Among such breaches could be action by the government of Iraq seriously to obstruct or impede the inspectors, to intimidate witnesses, or a pattern of behaviour where any single action appears relatively minor but the action as a whole add up to something deliberate and more significant: something that shows Iraq's intention not to comply'. If that is right, then the question is who makes the assessment of what constitutes a sufficiently serious breach. In the United Kingdom's view of the revival argument (though not the United States view) that can only be the Council, because only the Council can decide if a violation is sufficiently serious to revive the authorisation to use force.

18. It is right to say, however, that such an argument has less force if operative paragraph 4 operates automatically. Thus, the wording of operative paragraph 4 indicates that any failure by Iraq to comply with and cooperate fully in the implementation of the resolution will constitute a further material breach (leaving aside the question of whether false statements or omissions in the operative paragraph 3 declaration is an additional requirement). If operative paragraph 4 means what it says: the words 'cooperate fully' were included specifically to ensure that any instances of non-cooperation would amount to a further material breach. This is the United States analysis of operative paragraph 4 and is undoubtedly more consistent with the view that no further decision of the Council is necessary to authorise force, because it can be argued that the Council has determined in advance that any failure will be a material breach.

19. It has been suggested that it is possible to establish that Iraq has failed to take its final opportunity through the procedures in operative paragraphs 11 and 12 without regard to operative paragraph 4, in which case it is unnecessary to consider the effect of the words 'for assessment'. I do not consider that this argument really assists. First, the resolution must be read as a whole. Second, I accept that it is possible that a Council discussion under operative paragraph 12 may be triggered by a report from Blix and El-Baradei under operative paragraph 11 and that this may have the effect of establishing that Iraq has failed to take the final opportunity granted

by operative paragraph 2. But I do not consider that it can be argued seriously that operative paragraph 4 does not apply in these circumstances. It is clear from a comparison of the wording of paragraphs 4 and 11 that any Iraqi conduct which would be sufficient to trigger a report from the inspectors under operative paragraph 11 would also amount to a failure to comply with and cooperate fully in the implementation of the resolution and would thus also be covered by operative paragraph 4. In addition, the reference to paragraph 11 in operative paragraph 4 cannot be ignored. It is not entirely clear what this means, but the most convincing explanation seems to be that it is a recognition that an operative paragraph 11 inspectors' report would also constitute a report of further material breach within the meaning of operative paragraph 4 and would thus be assessed by the Council under operative paragraph 12. Moreover, the United States see operative paragraph 4 as an essential part of the mechanism for establishing that Iraq has failed to take its final opportunity.

20. It has also been suggested that the final words of operative paragraph 4 were chosen carefully to avoid the implication that it was for the Security Council to assess whether Iraqi conduct constituted a further material breach. The French proposed to amend operative paragraph 4 so that Iraqi conduct would only amount to a further material breach 'when assessed' as such by the Council, but this amendment was not accepted. I am not wholly convinced by this argument: if, for the reasons discussed in paragraph 17 above, operative paragraph 4 requires an assessment of Iraq's conduct by the Council, the alternative language makes little difference. However, I do accept that the negotiating history indicates that the words at the end of operative paragraph 4 'and shall be reported to the Council for assessment in accordance with paragraphs 11 and 12' were added at a late stage, but in substitution for other language which would clearly have had the effect of making any finding of further material breach subject to a further Council decision.

21. Whether a report comes to the Council under operative paragraph 4 or operative paragraph 11, the critical issue is what action the Council is required to take at that point. In other words, what does operative paragraph 12 require. It is clear that the

language of operative paragraph 12 was a compromise by the United States from their starting position that the Council should authorise in advance the use of all necessary means to enforce the cease-fire resolution in the event of continued violations by Iraq. It is equally clear, however, that the language does not expressly provide that a further Council decision is necessary to authorise the use of force. The paragraph indicates that in the event of a report of a further material breach (whether under operative paragraph 4 or operative paragraph 11) there will be a meeting of the Council to consider the situation and the need for compliance in order to secure international peace and security. The Council thus has the opportunity to take a further decision expressly authorising the use of force or, conceivably, to decide that other enforcement means should be used. But the Council might fail to act. The resolution does not state what is to happen in those circumstances. The clear US view is that, whatever the reason for the Council's failure to act, the determination of material breach in operative paragraphs 1 and 4 would remain valid, thus authorising the use of force without a further decision. My view is that different considerations apply in different circumstances. The operative paragraph 12 discussion might make clear that the Council's view is that military action is appropriate but that no further decision is required because of the terms of resolution 1441. In such a case, there would be good grounds for relying on the existing resolution as the legal basis for any subsequent military action. The more difficult scenario is if the views of Council members are divided and a further resolution is not adopted either because it fails to attract 9 votes or because it is vetoed.

22. The principal argument in favour of the view that no further decision is required to authorise force in these circumstances is that the language of operative paragraph 12 (ie 'consider') was chosen deliberately to indicate the need for a further discussion, but not a decision. As I have indicated, it is contended that this interpretation is supported by the negotiating history. The French and Russians both made proposals to amend operative paragraph 12 to include an express requirement for a further decision, but these proposals were not accepted. The US Administration insist that they made clear throughout that they would

not accept a text which subjected the use of force to a further Council decision. The French (and others) therefore knew what they were voting for. The US are confident that in accepting operative paragraphs 4 and 12, they were conceding a Council discussion and no more. The US, of course, approached the negotiation of resolution 1441 from a different starting point because, as I explained in paragraph 9 above, they have always taken the view that 'material breach' is a matter of objective fact and does not require a Security Council determination. (By contrast, the United Kingdom position taken on the advice of successive Law Officers, has been that it is for the Security Council to determine the existence of a material breach of the cease-fire.) Therefore, while the US objective was to ensure that the resolution did not constrain the right of action which they believed they already had, our objective was to secure a sufficient authorisation from the Council in the absence of which we would have had no right to act. I have considered whether this difference in the underlying legal view means that the effect of the resolution might be different for the United States than for the United Kingdom, but I have concluded that it does not affect the position. If operative paragraph 12 of the resolution, properly interpreted, were to mean that a further Council decision was required before force was authorised, this would constrain the United States just as much as the United Kingdom. It was therefore an essential negotiating point for the United States that the resolution should not concede the need for a second resolution. They are convinced that they succeeded.

23. I was impressed by the strength and sincerity of the views of the US Administration which I heard in Washington on this point. However, the difficulty is that we are reliant on their assertions for the view that the French (and others) knew and accepted that they were voting for a further discussion and no more. We have very little hard evidence of this beyond a couple of telegrams recording admissions by French negotiators that they knew the United States would not accept a resolution which required a further Council decision. The possibility remains that the French and others accepted operative paragraph 12 because in their view it gave them a sufficient basis on which to argue that a second resolution was required (even if that was not made expressly clear). A further difficulty is that, if the matter ever came

The Dodgiest Dossier

before a court, it is very uncertain to what extent the court would accept evidence of the negotiating history to support a particular interpretation of the resolution, given that most of the negotiations were conducted in private and there are no agreed or official records.

24. The counter view of operative paragraph 12 is that this paragraph must imply a decision by the Council. Three particular arguments support that approach:
(i) when taken with the word 'assessment' in operative paragraph 4, the language of operative paragraph 12 indicates that the Council will be assessing the seriousness of any Iraqi breach; this is especially powerful if in truth some assessment is necessary;
(ii) there is a special significance in the words 'in order to secure international peace and security'. They reflect not only the special responsibility of the Security Council under Article 39 of the UN Charter ('The Security Council shall determine the existence of any threat to the peace, breach of the peace, or acts of aggression and shall make recommendations, or decide what measures shall be taken to maintain or restore international peace and security'), but also pick up the language of both resolution 678 (which authorised the use of force 'to restore international peace and security in the area') and resolution 687 (which referred to the objective of 'restoring international peace and security in the area as set out in its recent resolutions'). The clear inference, it will be argued, is that this shows the Council was to exercise a deliberative role on that issue, ie to determine what it is necessary to secure international peace and security;
(iii) any other construction reduces the role of the Council discussion under operative paragraph 12 to a procedural formality. Others have jibbed at this categorisation, but I remain of the opinion that this would be the effect in legal terms of the view that no further resolution is required. The Council would be required to meet, and all members of the Council would be under an obligation to participate in the discussion in good faith, but even if an overwhelming majority of the Council were opposed to the use of force, military action could proceed regardless.

25. Where the meaning of a resolution is unclear from the text, the

statements made by members of the Council at the time of its adoption may be taken into account in order to ascertain the Council's intentions. The statements made during the debate on 8 November 2002 are not, however, conclusive. The United States and United Kingdom stated that further breaches would be reported to the Council 'for discussion'. Jeremy Greenstock then added that we would then expect the Council to 'meet its responsibilities', although (implicitly) we would be prepared to act without Council backing to ensure that the task of disarmament is completed. Only the United States explicitly stated that it believed that the resolution did not constrain the use of force by States to enforce relevant United Nations resolutions and protect world peace and security regardless of whether there was a further Council decision. Conversely, two other Council members, Mexico and Ireland, made clear that in their view a further decision of the Council was required before the use of force would be authorised. Syria also stated that 'the resolution should not be interpreted, through certain paragraphs, as authorising any State to use force'. Most other Council members were less clear in their comments. The joint statement of France, Russia and China is somewhat opaque, but seems to imply that a further decision is required. Many delegations welcomed the fact that there was 'no automaticity' in the resolution with regard to the use of force. But it is not clear what they meant by this. It could indicate that they did not consider that the resolution authorised the use of force in any circumstances by means of the revival argument. On the other hand there is some evidence from the negotiating history that their main concern was that the resolution should not authorise force immediately following its adoption on the basis of 'material breach' in operative paragraph 1 plus 'serious consequences' in operative paragraph 13. The United Kingdom and United States indicated that 'no automaticity' meant that there would be a Council discussion before force was used.

SUMMARY

26. To sum up, the language of resolution 1441 leaves the position unclear and the statements made on adoption of the resolution suggest that there were differences of view within the Council as to the legal effect of the resolution. Arguments can be made on both sides. A key question is whether there is in truth a need for an assessment of whether

Iraq's conduct constitutes a failure to take the final opportunity or has constituted a failure fully to cooperate within the meaning of **operative paragraph** 4 such that the basis of the cease-fire is destroyed. If an assessment is needed of that sort, it would be for the Council to make it. A narrow textual reading of the resolution suggests that sort of assessment is not needed, because the Council has pre-determined the issue. Public statements, on the other hand, say otherwise.

27. In these circumstances, I remain of the opinion that the safest legal course would be to secure the adoption of a further resolution to authorise the use of force. I have already advised that I do not believe that such a resolution need be explicit in its terms. The key point is that it should establish that the Council has concluded that Iraq has failed to take the final opportunity offered by resolution 1441, as in the draft which has already been tabled.

28. Nevertheless, having regard to the information on the negotiating history which I have been given and to the arguments of the US Administration which I heard in Washington, I accept that a reasonable case can be made that resolution 1441 is capable in principle of reviving the authorisation in 678 without a further resolution.

29. However, the argument that resolution 1441 alone has revived the authorisation to use force in resolution 678 will only be sustainable if there are strong factual grounds for concluding that Iraq has failed to take the final opportunity. In other words, we would need to be able to demonstrate hard evidence of non-compliance and non-cooperation. Given the structure of the resolution as a whole, the views of UNMOVIC and the International Atomic Energy Agency will be highly significant in this respect. In the light of the latest reporting by UNMOVIC, you will need to consider extremely carefully whether the evidence of non-cooperation and non-compliance by Iraq is sufficiently compelling to justify the conclusion that Iraq has failed to take its final opportunity.

30. In reaching my conclusions, I have taken account of the fact that on a number of previous occasions, including in relation to Operation

Desert Fox in December 1998 and Kosovo in 1999, UK forces have participated in military action on the basis of advice from my predecessors that the legality of the action under international law was no more than reasonably arguable. But a 'reasonable case' does not mean that if the matter ever came before a court I would be confident that the court would agree with this view. I judge that, having regard to the arguments on both sides, and considering the resolution as a whole in the light of the statements made on adoption and subsequently, a court might well conclude that operative paragraphs 4 and 12 do require a further Council decision in order to revive the authorisation in resolution 678. But equally I consider that the counter view can be reasonably maintained. However, it must be recognised that on previous occasions when military action was taken on the basis of a reasonably arguable case, the degree of public and Parliamentary scrutiny of the legal issue was nothing like as great as it is today.

31. The analysis set out above applies whether a second resolution fails to be adopted because of a lack of votes or because it is vetoed. As I have said before, I do not believe that there is any basis in law for arguing that there is an implied condition of reasonableness which can be read into the power of veto conferred on the permanent members of the Security Council by the United Nations Charter. So there are no grounds for arguing that an 'unreasonable veto' would entitle us to proceed on the basis of a presumed Security Council authorisation. In any event, if the majority of world opinion remains opposed to military action, it is likely to be difficult on the facts to categorise a French veto as 'unreasonable'. The legal analysis may, however, be affected by the course of events over the next week or so, eg the discussions on the draft second resolution. If we fail to achieve the adoption of a second resolution, we would need to consider urgently at that stage the strength of our legal case in the light of circumstances at that time.

POSSIBLE CONSEQUENCES OF ACTING
WITHOUT A SECOND RESOLUTION
32. In assessing the risks of acting on the basis of a reasonably arguable case, you will wish to take account of the ways in which the matter

might be brought before a court. There are a number of possibilities. First, the General Assembly could request an advisory opinion on the legality of the military action from the International Court of Justice. A request for such an opinion could be made at the request of a simple majority of the States within the General Assembly, so the United Kingdom and United States could not block such action. Second, given that the United Kingdom has accepted the compulsory jurisdiction of the International Court of Justice, it is possible that another State which has also accepted the Court's jurisdiction might seek to bring a case against us. This, however, seems a less likely option since Iraq itself could not bring a case and it is not easy to see on what basis any other State could establish that it had a dispute with the United Kingdom. But we cannot absolutely rule out that some State strongly opposed to military action might try to bring such a case. If it did, an application for interim measures to stop the campaign could be brought quite quickly (as it was in the case of Kosovo).

33. The International Criminal Court at present has no jurisdiction over the crime of aggression and could therefore not entertain a case concerning the lawfulness of any military action. The ICC will however have jurisdiction to examine whether any military campaign has been conducted in accordance with international humanitarian law. Given the controversy surrounding the legal basis for action, it is likely that the Court will scrutinise any allegations of war crimes by UK forces very closely. The Government has already been put on notice by CND that they intend to report to the ICC Prosecutor any incidents which their lawyers assess to have contravened the Geneva Conventions. The ICC would only be able to exercise jurisdiction over United Kingdom personnel if it considered that the UK prosecuting authorities were unable or unwilling to investigate and, if appropriate, prosecute the suspects themselves.

34. It is also possible that CND may try to bring further action to stop military action in the domestic courts, but I am confident that the courts would decline jurisdiction as they did in the case brought by CND last November. Two further, though probably more remote possibilities, are an attempted prosecution for murder on the grounds that the military

action is unlawful and an attempted prosecution for the crime of aggression. Aggression is a crime under customary international law which automatically forms part of domestic law. It might therefore be argued that international aggression is a crime recognised by the common law which can be prosecuted in the UK courts.

35. In short, there are a number of ways in which the opponents of military action might seek to bring a legal case, internationally or domestically, against the United Kingdom, members of the Government or UK military personnel. Some of these seem fairly remote possibilities, but given the strength of opposition to military action against Iraq, it would not be surprising if some attempts were made to get a case of some sort off the ground. We cannot be certain that they would not succeed. The General Assembly route may be the most likely, but you are in a better position than me to judge whether there are likely to be enough States in the General Assembly who would be willing to vote for such a course of action in present circumstances.

PROPORTIONALITY

36. Finally, I must stress that the lawfulness of military action depends not only on the existence of a legal basis, but also on the question of proportionality. Any force used pursuant to the authorisation in resolution 678 (whether or not there is a second resolution):
– must have as its objective the enforcement of the terms of the cease-fire contained in resolution 687 (1990) and subsequent relevant resolutions;
– be limited to what is necessary to achieve that objective; and
– must be a proportionate response to that objective, i.e. securing compliance with Iraq's disarmament obligations.

That is not to say that action may not be taken to remove Saddam Hussein from power if it can be demonstrated that such action is a necessary and proportionate measure to secure the disarmament of Iraq. But regime change cannot be the objective of military action. This should be borne in mind in considering the list of military targets and in making public statements about any campaign.

ATTORNEY GENERAL
7 March 2003

XI
A Principled Resignation

Eleven days later, on 18 March, the deputy legal adviser to the Foreign Office, Elizabeth Wilmshurst, resigned because she did not believe the war with Iraq was legal. Her letter was released by the Foreign Office to the BBC News website under the Freedom of Information Act.

A minute dated 18 March 2003 from Elizabeth Wilmshurst (Deputy Legal Adviser) to Michael Wood (The Legal Adviser), copied to the Private Secretary, the Private Secretary to the Permanent Under-Secretary, Alan Charlton (Director Personnel) and Andrew Patrick (Press Office):

1. I regret that I cannot agree that it is lawful to use force against Iraq without a second Security Council resolution to revive the authorisation given in SCR 678. I do not need to set out my reasoning; you are aware of it.

[The following italicised section was removed by the Foreign Office but later obtained by Channel 4 News]

My views accord with the advice that has been given consistently in this office before and after the adoption of UN security council resolution 1441 and with what the attorney general gave us to understand was his view prior to his letter of 7 March. (The view expressed in that letter has of course changed again into what is now the official line.)

I cannot in conscience go along with advice – within the Office or to the public or Parliament – which asserts the legitimacy of military action without such a resolution, particularly since an unlawful use of force on such a scale amounts to the crime of aggression; nor can I agree with such action in circumstances which are so detrimental to the international order and the rule of law.

2. I therefore need to leave the Office: my views on the legitimacy of the action in Iraq would not make it possible for me to continue my role as a Deputy Legal Adviser or my work more generally. For example in the context of the International Criminal Court, negotiations on the crime of aggression begin again this year. I am therefore discussing with Alan Charlton whether I may take approved early retirement. In case that is not possible this letter should be taken as constituting notice of my resignation.

3. I joined the Office in 1974. It has been a privilege to work here. I leave with very great sadness.

Afterword
Questions for President Bush

More than 560,000 people have already signed the letter to President Bush initiated by Representative John Conyers, Jr. It asks probing questions arising from the Downing Street Memo. As of early July 2005, no answer had been received to this, or to the earlier letter of 5 May, signed by 89 Members of Congress, which asked the same questions.

The Honorable George W. Bush
President of the United States of America
1600 Pennsylvania Ave, N.W.
Washington, D.C. 20005

Dear Mr. President:
We the undersigned write because of our concern regarding recent disclosures of a Downing Street Memo in the London *Times*, comprising the minutes of a meeting of Prime Minister Tony Blair and his top advisers. These minutes indicate that the United States and Great Britain agreed, by the summer of 2002, to attack Iraq, well before the invasion and before you even sought Congressional authority to engage in military action, and that US officials were deliberately manipulating intelligence to justify the war.

Among other things, the British government document quotes a high-ranking British official as stating that by July 2002, Bush had made up his mind to take military action. Yet, a month later, you stated you were still willing to 'look at all options' and that there was 'no timetable' for war. Secretary of Defence, Donald Rumsfeld, flatly stated that '[t]he president has made no such determination that we should go to war with Iraq.'

In addition, the origins of the false contention that Iraq had weapons of mass destruction remain a serious and lingering question about the lead up to the war. There is an ongoing debate about whether this was the result of a 'massive intelligence failure,' in other words a mistake, or the result of intentional and deliberate manipulation of intelligence to justify the case for war. The memo appears to resolve that debate as well, quoting the head of British intelligence as indicating that in the United States 'the intelligence and facts were being fixed around the policy.'

As a result of these concerns, we would ask that you respond to the following questions:

1) Do you or anyone in your administration dispute the accuracy of the leaked document?

2) Were arrangements being made, including the recruitment of allies, before you sought Congressional authorization to go to war? Did you or anyone in your Administration obtain Britain's commitment to invade prior to this time?

3) Was there an effort to create an ultimatum about weapons inspectors in order to help with the justification for the war as the minutes indicate?

4) At what point in time did you and Prime Minister Blair first agree it was necessary to invade Iraq?

5) Was there a coordinated effort with the US intelligence community and/or British officials to 'fix' the intelligence and facts around the policy as the leaked document states?

These are the same questions 89 Members of Congress, led by Rep. John Conyers, Jr., submitted to you on May 5, 2005. As citizens and taxpayers, we believe it is imperative that our people be able to trust our government and our commander in chief when you make representations and statements regarding our nation engaging in war. As a result, we would ask that you publicly respond to these questions as promptly as possible.

Thank you for your prompt attention to this matter.

THE SPOKESMAN
Founded by Bertrand Russell

Apocalypse Soon

Disaster Capitalism
Naomi Klein

Countering Civil Rights
Tony Bunyan

Apocalypse Soon
Edited by Ken Coates

Disaster Capitalism - **Naomi Klein**

Not Fit To Be Prime Minister
John Humphrys, Tony Blair, Reg Keys

Curveball - **Laurence H. Silberman & Charles S. Robb**

Iraq and the UN - **Hans von Sponeck**

A Sense of Proportion
Ralph Steadman

Countering Civil Rights - **Tony Bunyan**

Dossier
World Tribunal on Iraq
Removing America's Nuclear Weapons

Issue 86   £5.00

Albert Einstein, Bertrand Russell
Manifesto 50
Edited by Ken Coates

Requiem - **Kurt Vonnegut**

Building the Bomb - **Michele Ernsting, Joseph Rotblat & Ken Coates**

The Russell-Einstein Manifesto
Bertrand Russell & Albert Einstein

Convert & Disarm - **Seymour Melman**

The First Fireball - **John Berger**

Doctrines & Visions - **Noam Chomsky**

Dossier
Hiroshima Mayor's Call to Europe
Vanunu, Israel & Nuclear Proliferation

£5.00   Issue 85

One year's subscription to *The Spokesman* (4 issues) costs £20 (£25 ex UK)
Credit/Debit cards accepted - Spokesman Books (LRB), Russell House, Bulwell Lane, Nottingham, NG6 0BT, England Tel: 0115 9708318 - **Fax:** 0115 9420433
e-mail: elfeuro@compuserve.com | www.spokesmanbooks.com
"I've just had chance to read *The Spokesman*... it's really first-rate." **Noam Chomsky**

A Case to Answer
A first report on the potential impeachment of the Prime Minister for High Crimes and Misdemeanours in relation to the invasion of Iraq. Produced for Adam Price MP by Glen Rangwala and Dan Plesch
ISBN 0 85124 704 0 £5

Not Fit To Be Prime Minister?
John Humphrys interviews Tony Blair, with a commentary by Ken Coates.
ISBN 0 85124 709 1 £2

Tony Blair: The Old New Goes to War
Ken Coates discusses the emergence of New Labour. In addition, there are three case studies of how international law has been undermined by the outbreak of war on Iraq. They concern torture; the censored Iraqi Declaration about weapons of mass destruction produced in compliance with the requirements of UN Security Council Resolution 1441; and the Geneva Conventions on burying the war dead and treatment of prisoners.
ISBN 0 85124 679 6 £2

Straw Wars: Full Spectrum Sycophancy
Jack Straw's briefing for the Parliamentary Labour Party urging support for US preparations for fighting war from space, with a critical commentary by Ken Coates, plus the full text of *Vision for 2020*, which sets out the official military doctrine of US Space Command in the era when it seeks "Full Spectrum Dominance" of land, sea, air, space, and information.
ISBN 0 85124 659 1 £3

Available from Spokesman Books, Bertrand Russell House,
Bulwell Lane, Nottingham NG6 0BT, England.
Add 50p per item for postage.
phone 01159 708318 e-mail elfeuro@compuserve.com
www.spokesmanbooks.com
Cards accepted
Please make cheques payable to "Bertrand Russell House".